Lean Sales and Marketing

By Ade Asefeso MCIPS MBA

Second Edition

ISBN-13: 978-1499754179

ISBN-10: 1499754175

Publisher: AA Global Sourcing Ltd
Website: http://www.aaglobalsourcing.com

Table of Contents

Disclaimer

This publication is designed to provide competent and reliable information regarding the subject matter covered. However, it is sold with the understanding that the author and publisher are not engaged in rendering professional advice. The authors and publishers specifically disclaim any liability that is incurred from the use or application of contents of this book.

If you purchased this book without a cover you should be aware that this book may have been stolen property and reported as "unsold and destroyed" to the publisher. In this case neither the author nor the publisher has received any payment for this "stripped book."

Dedication

To my family and friends who seems to have been sent here to teach me something about who I am supposed to be. They have nurtured me, challenged me, and even opposed me.... But at every juncture has taught me!

This book is dedicated to my lovely boys, Thomas, Michael and Karl. Teaching them to manage their finance will give them the lives they deserve. They have taught me more about life, presence, and energy management than anything I have done in my life.

Chapter 1: Introduction

In all typical lean implementations there comes a time when the focus (and the pressure to change) moves to the Sales and Marketing functions. This is particularly the case in today's economic environment. Lean efforts in operations and support areas will result in a freeing up of capacity, as waste is eliminated and processes streamlined. Invariably the question that must be answered is "what to do with the available capacity?" All efforts must be made to resist the path of headcount reductions. Employees will no longer support the key concept of lean continuous improvement if they are concerned with job security. Of course, attrition is acceptable, but there must be more. An organization must leverage the available capacity in ways that create more value. To achieve this objective, Sales and Marketing personnel must identify opportunities within existing and new markets. This should be accomplished by utilizing existing sales and marketing resources in "smarter" ways in other words, by application of Lean Thinking. However, there has been strong resistance to the application of these common sense principles to Sales and Marketing. This book will explore the most common arguments, and provide a framework to apply Lean Thinking to these important functions.

The most common arguments involve the variable nature of, in particular, the Sales process. Sales professionals often take pride in the fact that "no customer is the same", "no sales situation is alike", etc. They often view the selling activity as "creative", and of course, "lean does not apply to creative processes". The independent nature of most people involved in selling is another challenge. In many cases, sales personnel are always "on the road", returning to the office only for periodic meetings. The result sometimes is the loss of a sense of belonging with co-workers, as well as a very real "disconnect" from important business processes in which they are involved. Many sales personnel take pleasure and pride in the independent nature of their position. This creates additional obstacles to overcome in the application of Lean.

Similar arguments are made about marketing processes, but to a much lesser extent. After all marketing is highly "creative". However, most marketing professionals recognize that the activities that they most often engage in are indeed processes to identify information needs; the sources of information; the means to analyze the information. What is often missing is the true ongoing management of the marketing process, as there tends to be a "project focus" to this function with marketing "campaigns" that by definition have a beginning and an end.

Standardizing "Creative Work"

At a company that creates marketing campaigns for consumer products, the argument being made was that standard work, and Lean in general, does not apply due to the creative nature of the process. However, the company realized during a value stream mapping exercise that up to 90% of what they do is really a process and a process that they very consistently follow, but failed to recognize. Market research, which is very process oriented and lends itself well to standardization, identifies the potential buyers of the products (e.g. males ages 18-49), as well as what media they frequent (e.g. radio, magazines). The only truly creative portion was the development of the radio spot which accounted for approximately 15% of the total process time, and 10% of the total lead time for the overall process. Once the company recognized this fact, they went forward in earnest to apply standard work to all of the non-creative processes and realized an overall lead time reduction of 40% and a process time reduction of 25%. The freed up capacity and improved customer service allowed them to be more responsive to ever changing needs of the customers with regard to marketing efforts.

The general lack of process focus must be overcome if an organization is to successfully apply lean concepts to the Sales and Marketing functions. The fact of the matter is you do not apply lean to functions, but rather to the activities that those functions perform. So, the necessary first step is to identify the activities that are regularly performed in these functions.

General Approach

In general, there are four basic steps: Stabilize, Standardize, Visualize, Improve (continuously). How you approach the application of lean depends on the "starting point". If a process is highly "unstable"- it has a very inconsistent and often unacceptable output; one must start to achieve some amount of stability. "Standardize" refers to the development of practices consistently followed by all people who perform the process and/or the activities within. Attempts to standardize an unstable process will in all likelihood provide undesirable results. However, if the process is stable, the focus can begin here to identify and agree on the best way to perform each activity or process. Once standardization has been achieved, providing "Visibility" to the process becomes the next focus. Of course, the ultimate goal is to "Improve" all processes on a continuous basis.

Stabilize

Instability is often caused by a complete lack of process definition. For example, Sales personnel are often left on their own to determine a process that works best for them in their regions of responsibility. However, this often has consequences such as inconsistent order related information across regions, extended "learning curves" for people assuming responsibility for a region, etc. Defining the process is often the key first step.

There exist numerous sales "models". All involve some variation of the following:
1. Identify new opportunities (typically through marketing efforts)
2. Follow-up on new opportunities and establish relationship (e.g. initial contact)

3. Identify customer needs (e.g. problems they are trying to solve) and buying parameters (e.g. budget, timing)
4. Identify customer decision making process (e.g. who, how, when)
5. Obtain Order
6. Post Sale follow-up

Each step represents a process that can be further defined, standardized, managed (even visually), and improved upon. Each organization should have a process that they can readily describe, and to which all Sales personnel can reference and commit.

In practice, most sales personnel are following something similar to this process, or at least particular steps, though they may not have thought of it in these terms. People will often overlook important steps simply due to a lack of process clarity, distractions, and other reasons. For example, many sales people overlook the "post sale" step, thereby missing out on the chance to identify future selling opportunities.

Very often it is simply a matter of putting on paper existing, poorly defined process steps, agreeing on terms and definitions, etc. The importance of this will be evident as we move on to "Standardize" and "Visualize". Once a selling process is in place, much needed stability can be achieved.

Standardize

It might help to think of the sales process previously described as "what to do" the steps that each

11

salesperson will follow. Standardizing refers to the "how" the manner in which the steps will be performed. Standard work is a foundation concept of lean. It includes the "key points" which define the "how" and the "why" to perform particular steps. Key points typically involve quality, efficiency, and time and timing. For example, a step must be performed in a particular way so as to insure an acceptable quality result. Sales personnel must fully complete order forms so that an order can be processes accurately. Order forms must be submitted at particular times so that they can be processed in a timely manner.

Defining the "how" and the "why" will better insure that sales personnel perform their activities in a way that meets the needs of "internal" customers (e.g. in-house order processors, scheduling personnel, and shipping). Sales personnel often overlook these needs in the rush to bring in orders. This just causes more non-value added processing waste even for the sales person who has to provide additional information at a later point. It is always better to do it right the first time. Selling is no different.

A distinction between standard work and "style" must be made here. Sales personnel often resist the concept of standard work because they confuse the two. The establishment of standard work does not mean that each sales person must practice the same style. Different styles can be exhibited while following standard processes. One sales person may establish rapport to build relationships by discussing subjects of personal interest, while another may

12

choose a different approach. Both can be effective, and both can still follow a standard selling process.

Further, standard work can be adjusted based on true customer needs. At one company the process time to be spent on a telephone call taking new orders was intentionally varied based on cultural differences of customers from the United States versus Europe. Customer surveys clearly identified that the customer's from Europe preferred more time on the telephone, while customers from the United States less. This was identified in standard work documentation. Order processors even newly hired ones following the established standard work could better insure a positive experience over time for customers from different regions of the world.

Tailoring Standard Work

One company did a lot of business with school districts in the United States. Different standard work had to be developed for several categories of school districts. For example, there were very real differences when dealing with school districts in the state of New Jersey where there are approximately 1,000 districts, and the state of Florida which has approximately 4.

Standard work needs to be applied to all of the "secondary" activities in which sales personnel are involved. Often overlooked is that the development of standard work, if done correctly, results in the streamlining of a process by identifying the most efficient and effective way to perform it. Travel planning, expense reporting, generating sales reports, etc. all of these activities need to be examined. Here lies tremendous opportunity to reduce non-value added processing waste. On average 10-15% of a sales person's time can be freed up by streamlining "secondary" activities. Valuable time can be gained that can be leveraged into proactive sales generation activities. Companies have realized a proportional 12-15% growth in sales from the previous year. These gains were not easy to obtain. It required a series of "cubicle level" kaizen events to identify the secondary activities, prioritize them, study them in detail, and determine ways to streamline.

Once there is agreement and commitment to defined standard work, the focus moves to "Visibility".

Visibility

Visual management is another key concept of lean. Visual communication has proven to be the most effective and efficient. After all nobody has much time to spare. Therefore, making key aspects of the process visible is self serving. Consider the benefits to the organization of making the following aspects of the sales process visible over time, perhaps in near real-time:

1. The activities that a sales person should be engaged in (e.g. prospecting, following up on new opportunities, following up on existing customers)
2. Non-standard conditions (e.g. not completing required activities when they were required, information quality issues that arise, spending

more or less time than a sales associate should on a particular activity)

3. Performance (e.g. not meeting personal or team goals, not processing new opportunities within a desired timeframe)
4. Queues of work (e.g. opportunities not being attended to by particular sales associates, quotes and orders not being processed in a timely manner)

If the entire sales organization had visibility to such conditions in the work environment, better decisions can be made and better actions taken. Too often sales organizations wait until the end of fiscal period when sales reports are generated to identify that problems arose with regard to performance. A lean enterprise has a very short "management timeframe" performance is frequently reviewed. However, it must be done in such a way that does not require a lot of non-value added effort such as generating time consuming reports. Providing visibility of the process is critical.

Today, many computer based sales systems provide work flow capability which can provide much needed visibility. The queue of sales opportunities at various stages of the process can be tracked by such tools. However, simpler methods can also be utilized. For example, developing standard work for the sales associate role defining the activities he or she is to perform, the time and/or timing of the activities (e.g. 2:00-3:00 each day), the number to be completed (e.g. five cold calls per day), and some visible evidence that the activity was complete will suffice. Office personnel can manually track the quality of information issued. All of this can often be accomplished via a simple dry erase board or boards in the sales office. Of course with the involvement of "outside" sales, electronic techniques tend to work better. Nonetheless, the use of simple, visible and worker managed techniques should not be overlooked.

Once processes have been standardized and made visible, the focus moves to continuous improvement.

Improvement

The role of the Sales Manager (and managers in general) must involve a significant portion of time (30-40%) directed to the improvement of the sales process and performance. Unfortunately, most sales managers today are involved in too many non-value added activities that take time away from this important. Based on the visual cues, the sales manager can identify opportunities for improvement, of overall processes or of individual performance. For example, if a sales associate is following established standard work and still not meeting performance expectations, this may become a focus of attention of the sales manager. The key here is that he or she is working already with standard conditions. Therefore, it should not take as much time to determine root causes for the problem. Another example might involve the "quality" of a particular sales associate. Perhaps he or she consistently submits incomplete or inaccurate information. This will become visible in a short time in a sales organization that is employing lean concepts. The sales manager can work with this person to correct the performance issue.

Yet another example involves the "mix" of activities that sales associates are expected to perform. Most people will put off particular activities which they do not care to perform. A sales associate may avoid making cold calls because it is unpleasant for them. After all it is much easier to call existing customers with whom a relationship already exists. However, important opportunities may be lost. The sales manager can work to address personal issues of this type in a timely manner with use of the visual techniques previously mentioned.

Improving performance of the sales team

A company previously had what could be described as a "sales funnel" where pre-qualified sales opportunities were placed in queue to be followed up upon at a later time. These opportunities were identified by geographical region in reality there were multiple "sales funnels". As part of a lean office effort, the organization made these queues visible. They also established goals with regard to the lead time in which they wanted to follow-up on these sales opportunities. Once this visibility was provided it became apparent that particular regions were not able to get to their opportunities in a timely manner. The sales performance measurement system was changed to be team based rather than individual. Sales management would monitor the regional queues and re-direct particular opportunities that were approaching the established lead time goal to sales associates who had available capacity. In other words, sales resources were "pulled" from other regions to meet demand in another region. This was a major contributor to the 12% one-year increase in revenue.

The application of lean concepts to the sales function, in particular standard work and visual management, can provide important benefits to the organization. By eliminating waste from the various sales related activities, valuable capacity can be freed up. This capacity can then be used to perform proactive sales generation activities. This increases the value that an organization delivers to its markets; the true goal of every lean enterprise.

However, this does not happen by chance. It is well thought out, with the involvement of the sales associates themselves throughout the application process. Therein is the biggest challenge for management to dedicate the necessary sales resources to kaizen activities for sufficient time to realize the important gains. This challenge is no different than that faced by all managers when implementing lean. Employee involvement in the improvement process is critical to success. The modest investment of time on the part of particular sales associates will be far exceeded by the benefits for the overall sales team.

Chapter 2: Lean Create Value for Customers

The starting point of all lean thinking is a clear and profound understanding of how we create value for the customers through our products and services. The sales and marketing personnel are in the vanguard of this vital aspect of lean.

While Sales and Marketing are often considered a separate topic, it is a mistake to think of these vital functions as of outside Lean Thinking.

Lean organizations focus on the first principle of lean, namely Customer Value.

The starting point of all lean thinking is a clear and profound understanding of how we create value for the customers through our products and services.

The sales and marketing personnel are in the vanguard of this vital aspect of lean.

Lean Accounting has a great deal of bearing on how effective these important aspects of the lean organization are.

Many of the characteristics of a lean approach to selling and marketing products and services are impacted by the value-based approach. If we recognize that a correct assessment and outworking of customer value is an important perhaps the most important aspect of lean thinking, then our approach to the customer will radically change. In reality, most companies have sales people who take a value-based approach intuitively. They recognize that to win new business and grow the company, it is vital to understand what creates value for our customers and to use this knowledge to develop appropriate products and services that maximize customer value.

They also recognize that prices must be based on the value created for the customer. While many companies continue to pursue the age-old fallacy of cost-plus pricing, savvy sales people recognize that the customer will only pay a price that matches the value the customer places on the products and services provided. Further, they know the customer does not care about what it costs us to make the product or provide the service. The only major exception to this rule is government contracting.

Government contracts are sometimes priced as a percentage uplift from the supplier's product costs; but even the government is moving away from this approach in recent years.

While many sales and marketing people intuitively address the customers and markets from a value viewpoint, lean organizations have standard and systematic methods of focusing on customer value throughout the entire organization and have methods to calculate the value created for the customer by the company's products and services. Customer value is widely understood throughout every aspect of the company's business is and is the primary driver of decisions and of lean improvement.

But, there are cases when the customer value focus is lost. In a recent article in The Wall Street Journal, a large well-known hospital system was bemoaning the fact that many of their patients come to the Emergency Room for treatment on weekends.

The hospital administrator stated that the Emergency Room treatment is much more expensive than a regular visit to the primary care clinic, and that these behaviours are undermining the hospital's ability to be financially viable. The administrator did not ask why the customers are coming at the weekend. It does not take a lean sensei to ask the question; "When is the most convenient time for a person working a regular job to visit the doctor?" This hospital works on a primary care schedule from 8:00am to 5:00pm Monday to Friday.

Obviously, the hospital's processes are set up for the convenience of the doctors and the administrators, not for value to the customer. This same hospital system has value stream maps carefully drawn and elegantly presented using complicated graphics software. Their value stream maps have detailed timings of how long it takes for each of the tasks required within the value stream. But there are no timings for the customers' experience. The hospital runs kaizen events to improve their processes and improvement is made, money is saved, and waste is eliminated. But is the customers' life improved? With regard to the customer's time no one knows because they do not take this into account when making improvements.

They do not even measure customer wait times or how long the customer has to sit in the doctor's office wearing an embarrassingly scanty gown while the doctor's attends to other "urgent issues."

Is it too simplistic to observe that industries with a record of very poor service to their customers often do not call a customer a "customer?" They use euphemisms like patient or passenger or tax-payer or (in the case of software) users or even seats.

This organization will not be successful with lean transformation if these attitudes persist. They are systemically violating the first principle of lean; value to the customer.

Lean thinking and improvement must be driven by a profound understanding of customer value; and in most cases this starts with the sales people and runs through to every process.

Chapter 3: Ways Lean Creates Value for Customers

Understanding the value created for the customer is the starting point of lean thinking; it is the first principle of lean.

The starting point for understanding customer value is the customers themselves. Lean organizations and lean sales professionals spend a great deal of time with their customers in order to understand their needs and how these needs can be translated into products and services.

There are many ways that value is created for a customer. Here are a few examples:

1. A superior product.
2. A unique product.
3. Converting commodity products into unique products through customization, innovation, or additional unique services.
4. A product that reduces the customer's costs or increases the customer's revenue.
5. A product that reduces cost or increases value for the customer's customer.
6. Providing a more complete solution to the customer's problem or need.
7. Lowering the life-cycle cost of ownership or use of the product.
8. Offering services only lean companies can provide; short lead time, reliability, perfect

quality, flexibility, lower inventories, improved cash flow, cooperative relationships, etc.

9. Creating esteem or prestige for your customer by being associated with your products and services

10. Providing very much superior services to the customer. "Give me exactly what I want, when I want it, how I want it, and where I want it. Solve my problem completely, treat me with respect, and charge me a fair price."

Once we understand how we create value for our customers then we can begin to quantify that value. These "value propositions" may well be different for different market segments and even for different customers. In most cases the starting point for the calculation of value to the customer is to know the baseline price i.e. the amount the customer is paying for the product or service your products and service replace or encompass. For example, if you are providing a better valve, then the starting point for value calculation is the cost of the values your customers currently uses.

When we know the baseline, then we can calculate the amount of savings or increased revenue created when the customer uses our products and services. Very often there are clear and "hard" financial benefits can be calculated. There may also be so-called "soft" benefits. These may involve relatively insignificant issues like convenience; or they may be important risk-reducing benefits like warranties or short lead times or exclusivity agreements. Others may involve the very substantial "soft" benefits that come from creating esteem for the customer by the use of your products.

These issues are more difficult to quantify and there is usually a need to work closely with the customers (and their customers) to understand the value created by these kinds of benefits. The starkest example of this is when your products create value by being fashionable. These benefits are quantified by obtaining information from the customer through surveys, market research, and by conducting pricing experiments.

Calculating a Value-Based Price

Once we have established the value created for the customers by our products and services, we can then move to calculating the price for the product. Here is an example. If the product creates £100 more value than the previous product that was priced at £200, then the question Is:

How much of the additional £100 will we keep and how much will we pass onto the customer?

This a pricing policy issue. We may decide to set a high price say £275 and recognize that at this price we may sell relatively fewer products but at the higher price. Alternatively we may price the product lower say £225 and hope to make less money on each individual product but make up for this by selling a much higher quantity. This is where a sound understanding of the price elasticity of demand is valuable.

Companies that have been using a more -or-less cost-plus approach to pricing often find it difficult to transfer their thinking towards a value-based approach. It takes some time before they are able to make these adjustments for their existing products, but as new products are introduced into their market places these can be priced based upon value. Gradually, pricing based on customer value will grow.

Advantages of Value-Based Pricing

The primary advantage of value-based pricing, as opposed to cost-plus pricing, is that your company will sell more products and usually at higher prices. In simple terms, there are two issues arising out of cost-plus pricing; either the sales people recognize that the price is too high and they do not win the business without considerable negotiation. Or the price asked for is lower than the sales people thought and they go for an easy sale. Either way; the company loses. The company sells a great number of the products that are under-priced and very few of the products that are over-priced.

On the other hand, companies using value-based pricing will set their prices based upon the true value to the customer and the company's pricing policy. The sales people are able to give their potential customers a logical rationale for the prices based upon the benefit the customer gains from using the product. This leads to higher revenues, higher profitability, a better informed and empowered sales force, and more harmonious customer relationships.

Chapter 4: Customer Partnerships

Lean organizations are not looking for one-time sales; they aim to create partnership relationships with their customers that build up and sustain over years. The issues we have just discussed in previous chapter of this book on value-based sales and marketing are very important to customer partnerships because partnership relies on mutual respect and shared benefit.

Rather than the debilitating power struggles between customer and supplier that is so common in Western industry, lean organizations seek to work cooperatively for mutual advantage.

Here is an example: an automotive component supplier understands that their customer needs to reduce the overall cost of the supply chain by 7% this year. The customer and supplier will then work together and use kaizen (continuous improvement) to eliminate waste and improve the processes across both of their organizations. The resulting cost reduction from making these improvements are then shared between the two organizations. There may or may not be any price reduction as such; it depends where the other savings occur. If they occur within the supplier then the financial benefit will be passed on into customer by price reductions. If the bulk of the cost savings occur within the customer, then the customer has achieved their cost reduction without the need for the supplier to reduce prices. Either way, there is mutual benefit for both supplier and customer.

It is evident that a company wishing to take this lean approach to customer relationships, cost saving, and pricing has to change the performance measurements on the purchasing processes.

Traditional companies focus strongly on standard costs and purchase price variance (PPV). This supports and motivates the toxic behaviours of many Western companies. Lean companies must eliminate these measurements and replace them with measurements that motivate cooperative relationships and lowest overall cost through process improvement and waste elimination.

It takes a long time to develop these kinds of cooperative relationships because they must be built on trust and respect. In much of Western industry there is a tradition of powerful customers coercing their suppliers for price reductions. This behaviour leads to the customer changing from one supplier to another to get a few pennies off the price. It leads to suppliers being forced to move production overseas to so-called "low cost" countries, and has lead to many suppliers being squeezed so hard that they fail and go into bankruptcy.

Think about behaviours of US car manufacturers in the 1990's and the 2000's. In response to increasing competition from companies like Toyota, Honda, Hyundai and others, they savagely squeezed their suppliers with the result mentioned above. The truly lean car manufacturers did the opposite. They allowed the suppliers to develop cooperative relationships and perhaps slowly but surely worked with them to eliminate waste and reduce the overall costs of their raw materials, components, and services. This has led to the curious paradox. If you are a patriotic American and wish to drive an all-American car, you must choose a Toyota or a Honda. Toyota and Honda cars that are assembled in America have the raw materials and components largely sourced within North American. The US car companies source the majority of their materials and components overseas rendering their automobiles to be largely foreign-made.

Why do Honda and Toyota take this partnership approach with their suppliers?

Because this is the low cost method. Buy locally and create long-term relationships. This is the lean way, and sales and marketing people within lean organizations must learn to give up the quick sale and work to create these long term relationships.

Chapter 5: Integrating Sales Into the Value Stream Organization

The sales process is the starting point for an order fulfilment value stream. Sales do not stand alone. Organizationally lean companies create value stream teams consisting of all the people, processes, and skills required to fulfil the customer needs and meet their demand. Whenever possible the sales people should be within these value stream teams, in the same way as production people, purchasing people, quality, materials handling, and so forth.

In many companies this approach is not practical. Often the sales teams need to be organized by markets, geography, or other pragmatic approaches. It usually makes no sense for a customer to have to deal with more than one sales person or sales team when they buy different kinds of products from the supplier. So the sales people are often organized differently from the order fulfilment value streams of which they are a part.

The ideal is for the sales people to be tightly integrated into the value stream team, but when this cannot be done directly; there must be methods for bringing the sales people and the order fulfilment value stream team into cooperative relationships.

Here are some of the methods employed:
   1. Cooperative opportunity assessment. When new, significant sales opportunities are

31

apparent it is important for the decisions related to these opportunities are done cross-functionally. Some companies develop opportunity assessment methods where the in-coming requests-for-quotes are filtered to identify significant opportunities. These opportunities are posted onto a visual board together with the relevant data. Over a period of a few days; using daily short stand-up style meetings; the sales people, purchasing, production, design, and other key people work cooperatively to address the opportunity and make decisions. These approaches have proven to lead to more sales, better pricing, faster response to the customer, and better strategic decisions.

2. Sales, Operations, and Financial Planning (SOFP) process. Lean organizations are very well planned companies. They have rigorous and formal (usually monthly) planning processes that are completed cross-functionally. The cross-functional teams include the sales people who provide sales forecasts for the future 12-18 months. The production people who provide capacity forecasts for the next 12-18 months, the new product development people providing information about when and how the new products will be introduced. And the financial people who provide financial information and create the financial forecasts that are an outcome of the planning of process. These groups work cooperatively together to create

the plan and then, after the planning process is complete, to fulfil the plan on their daily work.

3. Assign sales people to specific value streams even though they are not organizationally within the value stream team. The sales people work closely with the value stream teams to create cooperation with the sales organization, and to assist the value stream to make improvement, and solve problems.

Chapter 6: Sales and Marketing Teams in Lean Organizations

Many companies control their sales force; both internal sales people and external "reps" by individual compensation and commissions.

This method of compensation motivates the sales people to work independently to achieve the highest level of commissions. On the other hand, lean organizations are always looking to promote team-work. Team-work within the sales and marketing processes leads to sales teams that work together to address a market, geographical region, and/or product family. These companies may continue to remunerate their sales people based upon the sales they make, but these commissions are not paid based on individual contribution but team contribution.

These changes lead immediately to the sales people working together as a team to serve the customers and meet the company's sales needs.

Cooperative selling in most organizations is far more successful than individual selling in fulfilling the principles of lean thinking; filling customer needs for value, working in value streams, promoting flow at the pull of the customer, empowering the people, and pursuing perfection.

Consistent Sales Processes

Lean sales organizations work hard to develop standardized work within their teams. This leads to a consistent sales process that addresses their customers' value while increasing the company's revenues and profitability. Having consistent sales processes also leads to consistent performance from the customer's viewpoint, and enables the development of long-term customer relationships.

Performance Measurements that Drive Lean Behaviours

As with most lean changes, it is necessary to change the performance measurements used to control and improve the sales processes. In traditional companies the sales performance measurements are very much based around judging the individual sales person. Lean performance measurements will focus on the processes that create excellent sale results. These measurement changes together with a value-based approach lead to radical changes to the way sales and marketing happen in lean companies.

Demand Management

As discussed previously, the sales and marketing teams in lean organizations are very closely involved in the planning process, SOFP. This means the sales and marketing teams are not merely providing forecast information but are an important part of the cross-functional teams that make the short-term and long-term planning decisions.

One important outcome of the SOFP (Sales, Operations and Financial Planning) process is a level schedule of production, service provision, product development processes, and demand on suppliers. The ability to create a predictable and orderly working environment is critical to creating highly productive value stream processes. In many companies there are sales policies that militate against a level schedule. These include providing customers with discounted prices for large orders; leading to spikes of demand that do not fit well into lean production. Similarly, companies that press heavily on their people to achieve the budgeted month-end and quarter-end results usually manage to undermine their lean transformation. If a sales person or team is motivated strongly to achieve month-end or quarter-end sales revenues based upon a budgeted goal, then the sales team will work hard to achieve it. But this will often be achieved by bringing in sales that are not linear.

One company we work with stated that they are a lean company for 3 weeks of the month. When the 4th week comes around they are forced to revert to the traditional month-end tricks to meet the budgeted goals. Lean companies use methods that are the opposite of these because they want to promote lean flow and stable production. Instead if rewarding customers that place large batch orders lean organizations apply discounts to motivate many smaller orders. It is better for a lean company to receive small orders daily than to get a large monthly order. The company's sales and promotional methods change to motivate small, frequent orders. Similarly, some companies provide discounts to the customers that place orders linearly over the year or quarter. Other companies provide bonuses to sales teams that bring in linear orders from their customers.

Target Costing

The purpose of target costing is to drive the company's lean change and improvement directly from customer value. This requires a deep understanding within the value stream of the value created for the customer by the value stream products and processes. From this we can move to calculating the price of the product and the target cost required to meet the customers' needs for value while satisfying our own needs for profitability and cash-flow and fulfil the company's short and long-term goals.

We then split the target cost into sections according to the materials costs and the various major sub-assemblies manufactured during the value streams process. This leads to a process that is fundamentally lean; continuous improvement within the value stream is directly driven from customer value.

There are four major steps in the Target Costing process:
1. Understanding customer needs.
2. Quantifying customer needs.
3. Calculating target costs.
4. Attaining target costs through continuous improvement

The first two steps are similar to the process for calculating customer value, described previously. Once we know the value we can assess the price of the product in our various markets. The product target cost is then calculated by subtracting the required profitability from the price. The fourth step is to systematically and relentlessly use this information to drive continuous improvement throughout our processes to bring the costs into line with the target costs and to create superior value for the customers.

Kaizen - Continuous Improvement

Everyone in a lean organization is required to make operational improvement to their processes using a series of lean improvement and problem solving methods.

Sales and marketing is not an exception. The sales and marketing people are required to achieve 5S, and to do kaizen events to improve their own processes. Once the local improvements have been achieved, then sales and marketing people will work with the value stream teams to improve the order fulfilment process and integrate the sales activities more closely. Sales and marketing people also participate in kaizen improvement efforts throughout the organization. Very often they take the role of "fresh eyes"; the people in the value stream team with no direct knowledge of the process being improved but who can ask the direct questions and provide a broader business view. They also enable the teams to be more focused on customer value.

39

Many companies make serious mistakes when they approach the transformation to a lean organization. One of these mistakes is to think of lean as a manufacturing issue. Lean manufacturing cannot succeed unless all other aspects of the business are similarly transformed by lean thinking. In our experience sales and marketing are the most neglected parts of the business by companies claiming to be "going lean." As with other business processes, sales and marketing in most companies needs to be radically changed for lean to be successful. The focus must move to customer value, the sales people must work in teams, create customer partnerships, create even flow of demand, use standardized work, and apply continuous improvement to every aspect of their work.

Chapter 7: How We Put It Together Sets Us Apart

Several years ago, I was the guest speaker at the National Sales Meeting for a very large technology company. The theme they had selected for the meeting and the year was, "its how we put it together that sets us apart!"

This is actually a core concept to Lean and very important as we think about applying these principles to Lean Sales and Marketing. It's also an area that deserves many more attention, so this is just the starting point.

Organizations that really understand and apply Lean, understand that Lean is a "systems or holistic approach." While we may be focused on a specific problem area, we miss a huge benefit to Lean. In fact by isolating what we do to one component, we are probably only addressing that component and may not be addressing root problems. Too often, we break things into components, optimizing the components, yet sub-optimizing the performance of the entire organization. IT may be delivering a perfectly implemented CRM tool, but it makes the sales person's job more difficult, reducing their sales time. Marketing could be implementing a perfect lead development programs, but could be overwhelming sales who don't have the ability to follow up the leads.

We see these piecemeal approaches to solving problems all the time. For example, the sales training program that is not integrated into the systems processes and tools the sales people use. Or the training program than has no follow on reinforcement or management coaching. Most of these may have a very short impact, but seldom have a sustained performance impact. Likewise, the latest greatest Sales 2.0 tool, that is implemented without a real understanding of how it impacts the day to day life of the sales professional. Or the compensation system that fails to produce the results expected.

Or we see problems in the interrelationship and effective operations of functions. Marketing and sales may not be aligned in priorities. Marketing may be optimizing performance that enables it to achieve its objectives, yet could have an impact on sales. Or sales optimize what it does without consideration of the impact on sales. Boundaries and silos can isolate or disguise problems. Without looking at things as a whole, we may be missing opportunities. We may not be using our resources as effectively as possible, maximizing our collective impact on the customer.

I could go on and on. Just like a manufacturing system, a high performance sale requires understanding how all the components (people, process, programs, tools, incentives/metrics, training, etc.) all interrelate. If we are applying Lean principles to what we do as sales and marketing professionals, we need to simultaneously look at the components, but we also need to look at how they interrelate and work together. We may choose to sub-optimize one element, if by doing this, we have a positive impact on the whole organization.

There is another aspect of "How We Put It All Together" that's really important. It has to do with the customer experience that we create not only with the customer's buying experience, but with their whole experience in working with us; how they order, receive and implement the products; our contracts and billing; the customer service, repair, and warranty experiences; even their perception of what we stand for or what we do in the community and markets. It could be their whole experience as we "nurture" and work with them through their buying process. Each thing we do reinforces the customer view of us. All of these shape an influence the customer's views of us and their willingness to buy.

Too often, we forget this; we focus on the product only and not leveraging the total customer experience. We focus on the product, its features and functions. We neglect all the other elements of their experience, failing to leverage them in selling and the ongoing relationship. Lean focuses us to focus on the whole experience and the total value we create through that experience.

Lean, also, when we look at things from a total system point of view gives us tremendous competitive advantage. The differentiation between our products and those of the competition may be very small (or we may sell a commodity) Lean companies know the product is just one component of what their customers buy.

Being Lean provides great competitive positioning and differentiation. Our competitors may try to copy what we do. They can copy our products; they can copy our pricing or even discount. They can try to emulate many of the pieces-parts. What they miss, however, is that it's virtually impossible to copy the whole thing. At best they are a poor facsimile, which our customers need to understand.

Lean companies look at competition differently. They care about the competition, but don't seek to copy or emulate the competition. They try to understand the value their competitors create and what it means to customers and market. Lean companies use this to assess their own strategies and their own value creation. However, they are driven by their own creation strategies, the experience they want to create, and what they stand for in the markets and communities.

It's critical in how we look to constantly improve our customers' experiences and to how we compete and win. Lean provides us a path and tools to determine these and exploit them.

Chapter 8: Lean Sales and Marketing Kaizan Blitz

Over the past several weeks, I have had the good fortune to participate in a number of "Kaizen Blitz's" with a client. They were focused on identifying great improvements in their sales strategies. One of the profound things about these workshops was that 70% of the participants came from non-sales or marketing functions; manufacturing, development, operations, quality, legal, human resources, and executive management. The results of these meetings as we move forward in executing these ideas will drive tremendous improvement in the client's growth, with great improvements in the performance and productivity of sales and marketing.

Let me step back, a Kaizan Blitz is one of the processes or tools used as part of "Lean" approaches to the organization. We often hear of lean manufacturing, lean development, more recently of lean Start-ups and lean entrepreneurship, how today's entrepreneurs use continuous innovation to create radically successful businesses. Lean has its roots in the quality movement and most famously traced to the Toyota Production system. The kaizen sessions are focused workshops on continuous improvement, eliminating work that does not create value.

Many people mistake "Lean" as a process of eliminating unnecessary or wasteful work. In reality lean is focused on Value Creation. What Lean is really about is identifying the true essence of Creating Value. It requires that we focus on what is needed to create value, identifying everything that does not create value or diminishes value; all of that is considered waste. Through the process of implementing "Lean," the organization must constantly focus on identifying what value is and focusing 100% on those activities that create value.

In manufacturing, the downstream steps/activities and the people who performed them are the "customer." In lean manufacturing, we focus on making sure that we have eliminated all the non-value added things for those customers. For instance eliminating waste, reducing errors, maximizing efficiency, so the product we provide these downstream customers enables them to maximize the value they add for their downstream customers.

Lean is one of the most important concepts for us to understand and drive in Sales and Marketing. It mandates us to really understand what value is from the point of view of our customers, and to focus exclusively on activities that create value for the customer, eliminating everything else.

Lean is not a random approach to improving our ability to create and deliver value. It is based on the "scientific method." We analyze what value is, we analyze the steps and activities required to create and deliver value, we analyze and identify those activities that don't contribute to value and we eliminate them. We may create "experiments" to test what customers really value; they may not be able to articulate it, so we have to develop some "hypotheses," rapidly creating and executing experiments to test those hypotheses, iterating rapidly so we can accelerate our understanding of value and focus on value creation and delivery.

I want to go back, for a moment, to these Kaizen blitz's with my client. I mentioned that 70% of the participants came from outside sales and marketing. It's one of the important things we need to recognize about sales and marketing and "Lean" forces us to understand this. That is, Sales Revenue Generation is not just the job of sales people. It requires total alignment and support of the entire organization. Every function contributes to Revenue Generation. Maximizing our ability to create value for our customers is not just Sales and marketing's job, but requires the entire organization working together.

In these workshops, we identified what were the "wastes," the non value creating activities between these organizations that impact our ability to connect most effectively with our customers. We found huge numbers of activities, wasteful meetings, ill defined roles and responsibilities, an absence of accountability, an absence of measures. The teams now know what to focus on eliminating. One of the results of this effort is that the teams freed up the time and wasteful activities of sales people we established a goal of enabling sales people to spend 50% of their time with customers in value creating sales activities more than doubling the time they currently spend.

In the workshops, we started to go beyond eliminating waste, focusing on what "Lean" is really about, Value Creation. We have a long way to go in these projects, but we have identified some next steps. I will be writing about these, along with other aspects of "Lean Sales and Marketing" later in this book.

Chapter 9: Defining Value

As I typed the title I cringed. Somehow I feel the title is redundant. As I have mentioned in previously, Lean is about understanding the essence of what customers' value and focusing our efforts on creating and delivering that value. The key word in the last sentence is essence.

Too many times we really don't understand what our customers' value. We impose what we think they should value instead. Alternatively, we know what value our solutions provide, so we seek to impose these on them. We develop all sorts of marketing collateral with long lists of feature and benefits (the more sophisticated phrase these in long lists of value propositions).

Too often, there is the attitude that more is better. The longer the list of benefits we can create, the longer the list of "value" we deliver, the better. If our list is longer than the competition's, then clearly we create much greater value than they.

When we don't know, or are too lazy to figure it out, we substitute by imposing everything on the customer throwing all the value we create at them, hoping they can sort it out and determine our solutions create value for them.

More value is not better! More value is confusing and distracting. More value can create complexity from the point of view of the customer; they have to figure out and sort through all the stuff we throw at them. More value wastes customer time and resources in trying to understand exactly what value we create for the customer. More value, in the eyes of the customer becomes less value!

Lean requires us to understand the essence of what our customers' value. It requires us to focus everything on those few things that are critical to the customer. It means we don't waste their time or ours in talking about lots of other things they may represent value to others, but they don't represent value to this customer.

Understanding the essence of what customers' value simplifies things tremendously. Once we understand the essence of what customers' value, we focus everything around these elements, we don't waste our time or the customers' time on anything that is extraneous or non value add. In fact, we set ourselves apart by creating great clarity for the customer.

It's our job as sales and marketing professionals to determine what our customers' value, focusing everything on the essence of what they value. Implicitly, this means one to one. This means we have to understand what each customer each person values, then focus on creating that value with them. Marketing needs to segment, focusing on the value created for each segment. Our messaging needs to become more refined and more focused on smaller segments until eventually we define segments of one. Marketing probably doesn't deal with segments of one that is the role of the sales person, but marketing needs to provide sales the tools to be able to understand what each customer values then create that value for the customer.

It is wonderful if with each of our products and services, we have very long lists of value elements. These increase the likelihood that we can create value for many different customers. But it is pure laziness and absence of customer focus to impose all of them on the customer, increasing their work to figure it out. It's incumbent on us to focus, to eliminate on all those "value elements" the customer does not value, instead focusing on the essence of what they value.

Value creation is central to Lean Sales and Marketing. But Lean focuses on the customer understanding, creating and delivering what they value. Delivering great and differentiated value means focusing on the essence of what customers' value, not on delivering more value.

Chapter 10: The Role of Managers

Managers play a critical role in the lean sales and marketing organization. It is different from what we see in the traditional organization.

In the traditional organization, there's the belief that we work for our managers. We all know the corporate hierarchy and pyramid. In many organizations, managers spend too little time coaching. They are busy in meetings, they are busy with paperwork, and they don't have time or the skills to work with their people. Too often, they look for blame, rather than understanding and solving problems.

In the Lean Sales and Marketing organization, the pyramid is inverted. The role of the manager is very different.

In lean organizations, Managers serve their people. Managers create the work environment that enables people to perform. The manager removes barriers that impact the ability of sales people to do their jobs. Manager's developed and design processes that maximize performance. They determine the tools people need to perform at the highest levels possible. They make sure people understand what their job is, that they are trained and understand how to do their jobs. They constantly coach and develop their people's capabilities.

When there are problems, managers, step in to identify the problems and remove them. When problems occur, they don't blame the people and find fault with them. They look for problems in the process and try to remove them. Beating people up don't solve the problem; it disrespects the people and creates waste.

To be successful, managers must know the job their people perform. They must be able to do it well themselves.

All the way up (or in the lean perspective, down) the hierarchy, the role of the managers or executives is to serve and lead by example.

Chapter 11: Standard Work

I can imagine at least 70% of my readers shuddering at this concept. "There is nothing standard about what we do in sales; we have to be free to respond to the specific customer situation!" "Every customer situation is different; it can't be fit into a standard approach." "Sales is not like manufacturing! We don't do the exact thing over and over, the key is to adapt to the customer situation, to be nimble!"

Certainly, standard work in sales can never be as precisely defined as a manufacturing process. But the objections to "standard work" in sales are really just the excuses of those who aren't maximizing their productivity, effectiveness, and efficiency with the customer.

As we start to look at standard work within sales, we want to look focus on a couple of issues. How do we maximize the time sales people spend with customers helping them identify and solve problems? How do we maximize the impact and value of each interchange with the customer? We also need to look at how standard work improves our ability to be creative and innovate.

Maximizing the time sales people spend with customers.

A number of surveys say the time sales people spend on customer related sales activities is around 40%. In many of our own surveys. We find organizations and sales people where the time spent on customer focused, sales related activities are in the low 20's. Sales people both through their own behaviours and through time drains created in their organizations are spending more and more time in non customer, non sales related activities. Imagine the impact of being able to free up just 10% of a sales person's time. Changing nothing else, but giving a sales person currently spending 20% of their time in customer-sales related activities another 10% for a total of 30% has the potential of increasing sales by 50%!

The time drains are both self imposed (poor personal time management and avoidance behaviours), and organizationally imposed. Some of the organizationally imposed time drains are inadvertent poorly defined roles, responsibilities, accountabilities. For example, the customer has a problem or question; they don't know who to call, so they call the sales person. Or there is a poorly defined or unresponsive problem management process and the sales person gets sucked into managing the process.

Other organizationally imposed time drains come from the tremendous restructuring we see organizations go through. As organizations are down sized and jobs are eliminated, we fail look at the work that remains. Fewer people, the same amount of work, guess who picks up the slack; sales – sales wants to keep the customers happy, to get things done. With our changes in organization, we don't look at work that needs to be stopped or eliminated. Likewise, with mergers and consolidations. There are sometime duplicate, redundant efforts; we don't look at what is changed, what need to be done, who needs to do it, and what needs to be stopped.

The biggest organizationally induced category of time drains, wasted effort ends up being "this is the way we have always done things!" The world is different, customers needs are different, our organizations are different; we can no longer let the excuse of the way we have done things drive our behaviours; we simply don't have the time for that!

A lot of the time drains are personally induced simply bad time management or avoidance. We spend too much time on email; we let our days be interrupt driven rather than purposefully structured. We don't block time for prospecting, we don't commit to a goal for prospecting. We don't leverage the tools (Yes, CRM) to help improve our productivity time management and the quality of how we spend our time.

One of the biggest, we don't have or don't use our sales process, choosing instead to take a random walk wasting a lot of our customers' time and ours. The data shows that people and organizations that use a sales process consistently perform at much higher levels than those who don't. Just one data point from CSO Insights 2011 Sales Performance Optimization Study shows that in organizations where most of the sales people are leveraging the sales process, 70% beat their quotas, and in those where people are not consistently using the sales process on 51% beat their quotas.

The same report shows even more profound differences in the value those sales people create; 43% of those using the sales process clearly understand the customer buying process and are aligned with it compared to 6% for those that don't! 38% of those using the process can sell value and avoid discounting, where only 4% of those who have no sales process do the same!

The sales process is one of the most important elements of Standard Work we need to focus on. The difference in results is profound, so it is unimaginable that we don't define and consistently execute our sales process.

Closely related to this is another personally induced time drain, the lack of planning and preparation. Too often, we use the excuse of "busyness" to avoid planning. So we go into calls unprepared, we don't know what are the most important next steps in the deal, we don't take the time to analyze our pipelines, we don't have territory or account plans. We have plenty of time to recover from mistakes, but we never seem to have the time to plan then execute with precision. Opportunity/Deal Plans, Pipeline Management, Account/Territory Plans, Sales Call Plans are all forms of Standard Work. They help us focus, the help improve our ability to execute sharply; they help us use our time, and our customers' time as effectively as possible.

Maximize the value and impact of each exchange with the customer.

The essence of lean is about creating and delivering value. Lean focuses on the very essence of value not what we think is value, but on what the customer views as value. Any activity that does not create value is considered waste. Waste adds cost to us and to the customer. Lean seeks to identify and eliminate all non-value generating activities.

We can't create and deliver value unless we understand what our customers' value. Realistically, this is the process of really understanding the value we (individually and organizationally) can create and deliver, then finding those groups of customers (marketing calls them segments) that value what we do.

We waste our time and the customers" time calling outside our "sweet spot." Selling outside the sweet spot is pure wishful thinking and any results are more likely exceptions than patterns of success. So an element of Standard Work is clearly identifying our sweet spot, focusing all our activities within that sweet spot.

It takes great customer intimacy and knowledge to be able to define our sweet spot(s). It takes courage and discipline to focus on our sweet spot(s), but that's where we are most effective in value creation and delivery. If we want to be Lean in our sales and marketing efforts, we have to have that focus and discipline.

Our sales process is another important element of maximizing our value in every interchange with the customer. The sales process is based on our best experience in aligning how we sell with how customers buy. It focuses on identifying the critical activities and critical steps needed to help the customer buy. It should be driven by simplicity. It should seek to minimize activity and time focusing on the most important and eliminating all activities and steps that don't create value.

The sales process then becomes our road map, keeping us focused on activities we know to be value creating, and eliminating those that don't create value.

Likewise, planning keeps us focused on value creation. The simple act of creating a sales call plan (using our Standard Work, Sales Call Planning Template) forces us to think, "What value am I creating in this call?" If we can't answer the question, we should reschedule the meeting for a time when we can answer that question.

Standard work focuses our creativity and gives direction to our innovation.

Most often, when I talk about standard work, process and discipline, the biggest excuse is "It inhibits our creativity; it limits our ability to respond, to "dance" in front of the customer, to be nimble, to innovate." (Most of the time these excuses come from those who are the least creative, nimble and innovative.)

I believe that's just flat wrong. If we look at professions traditionally viewed as being "creative," art, music, dance, theatre, writing, even sports, we see great discipline, process focus, and "standard work."

As an example, I am a "wannabe" triathlete. Success in triathlons is not simply a matter of swimming, biking, running fast. I spend endless hours practicing and trying to perfect my swimming stroke, my pedalling stroke and position on the bike, my running stride. I try to find my ideal cadence and performance in each segment; I look at my power output and try to maintain constant power. My coach wants to make every motion, every effort count; they want to help me eliminate those efforts that waste energy. On the bike, I have a weird habit of moving my right knee outward on the upstroke. They are trying to help me straighten it out, it improves my power output, the outward motion wastes energy and power.

All creatives have their process, their standard work. In dance and athletics, top performers have no wasted motion. Every paint stokes or every note has purpose and meaning. Creatives constantly focus on the essence of creativity and innovation in their fields. They create their standard work and processes. They simultaneously look for precision in execution of that standard work, freeing themselves to be creative within those bounds. They also look for continually improving the standard work.

Getting Started

I have already talked about some areas of Standard Work, as starting points; here are some quick lists to get you started.

Primarily sales focused standard work.
1. Sales process.
2. Funnel/Pipeline process.
3. Opportunity/Deal strategy.
4. Call planning/execution.
5. Account planning.
6. Territory planning.
7. Sales reviews.
8. Daily/weekly calendaring/scheduling.
9. Prospecting.
10. Proposal development.
11. Reporting (Activity, deal, pipeline/forecasting, expense, etc.)
12. Training, onboarding.
13. Recruiting, hiring.
14. Commission reporting/management.
15. (There are more, but I'll stop here)

Non-sales but may require some sales engagement:
1. Project/program management.
2. Customer problem resolution/escalation.
3. Customer service (all areas; technical, billing, scheduling, shipping, information, repair, warranty, etc.)
4. Lead management, development.
5. Product introduction/launch.
6. Customer satisfaction/Net Promoter.
7. Customer communication/nurturing.

8. New product development and early customer involvement.
9. Cross organizational roles and responsibilities.
10. (Again, there are many more, but I'll stop here)

Each of these has large elements of Standard Work which optimize our ability to create and deliver value. Each of these has tremendous impact (positively and negatively) on sales time, productivity, and value creation. Look for your biggest areas of problems, attack one at a time, develop the standard work, train everyone, communicate more broadly, provide the tools to facilitate the execution, and ruthlessly measure.

Standard work is at the core of high performance and value creation.

We need to closely examine everything we do; our sales processes, how we spend our time, roles and responsibilities not only within sales but across the organization. We need to carefully understand those activities that create value, and those that don't. In my experience, simpler is usually better.

Chapter 12: Time Available for Selling

A sales person's job is to sell nothing surprising. More and more, however, it seems that things conspire against us, diverting us from engaging our customers. There's some market research that puts the time available for selling at around 42%, but more and more, that figure seems optimistic.

Several years ago, we did a study of a one of the largest telecommunications companies in the world. With their B2B sales people, we found time available for selling had slipped just below 20%. More recently, with several large clients, we found time available for selling in the range of 22-34%.

Regardless, which figures you look at, we spend the majority of our time not selling! Some of it is understandable and very important. We have to devote a certain amount of our time to administrative function like reporting, following up on customer related queries, internal meetings, and other things. Training, whether on new products, sales, or in other areas are important. Planning is critical and usually time well spent; it makes us more impactful when we are meeting with our customers. Then there is things we can't avoid; travel to and from customers.

These are all part of the job; they are things we have to do in order to sell. With each of these, however, we have to make sure we are using our time as effectively as possible. It's critical that we identify time drains. For example, so many of our internal meetings are wastes of time simply because there is no pre-published agenda, people aren't prepared, and people aren't "present" (This is the multitasking issue).

Some of our lost time is system or organizationally imposed, some of it is self-imposed or inflicted.

System or organizationally imposed time drains

As mentioned before, wasteful meetings are usually a huge source of wasted time. The absence of agendas, poor preparation and poor participation wastes hundreds of hours of our time every year taking away from the time we have to do what we are really accountable for.

There are some other more subtle system or organizationally imposed time drains. One of the biggest is poorly defined roles and responsibilities. For example, I am working with a company that has made a number of major acquisitions recently. In consolidating the acquisitions, they had reorganized the sales organization, consolidated the accounts and all the normal things. But they had done this really quickly, without really understanding the different business processes of the organizations they were smashing together. As a result, we found two things were happening; there were a lot of duplicated and redundant efforts that cause a lot of confusion to customers and within the organization. Also, there were a lot of things falling through the cracks. As a result, sales people were spending a lot of time "fixing" things, managing misunderstandings and mistakes, or masking the internal "disorganization" from the customers.

It's important to understand the systemic or organizationally imposed time drains. There are a couple of simple tools you can use to begin to understand these.

1. The first is clearly defining roles and responsibilities.
2. The second is workflow mapping. This may take a little more time but it's the old fashion flowcharting. Map how things get done, what the workflow are. Identify areas of waste and eliminate them, work to make them as efficient as possible. This takes a little longer but is very powerful, particularly when done as a team, with all the various people involved. One of the best things it does, is it gives everyone great insight into how the business works, what the critical workflow is, and where the problem areas are. Don't try to do all the workflows at one time, it can be overwhelming. Take one at a time, focusing on the highest priority or core workflows. The tools to do this are simple flow charting tools, or I really like using Mind Mapping tools to look at this.

Self imposed time drains

These are all on us! We all do them, consciously or unconsciously. They include just bad organization and time management. Not having an organized approach to things, not planning and prioritizing our time, being interrupt and reaction driven diverts us from achieving our objectives. Being undisciplined in the use of the time we have to sell by not leveraging our sales process, by not developing and executing focused deal strategies, by not planning and executing high impact sales calls all waste our time, that of our peers, and our customers' time.

Then there is avoidance; the excuses we use to put off doing things that we don't like. Putting off updating the CRM system, putting off that report, or the big one prospecting avoidance. People find all sorts of excuses to put these things off, and if we can't find one, there is always email.

These are in our own control. They rob us of tremendous amounts of time. They block us from achieving our goals. And we can fix them ourselves!

Productivity multiplier

Identifying and eliminating time drains are critical activities for high performance! Imagine, without changing how you sell, you can dramatically improve sales productivity. In the case of the telecommunications company I identified at the top of this chapter, in our first pass at identifying the time drains, we were able to help the sales force get from less than 20% time available to selling to more than 40%; we were able to more than double sales productivity without doing anything else (and there were a lot of other things that improved as well). And we were able to do this in less than 100 days! Later we were able to do much more, both in increasing time available for selling and improving sales effectiveness.

Finally
1. Do you know how much time you have available for selling?
2. Have you identified the systemic and organizationally imposed time drains? Are you working to eliminate them?
3. Have you identified the self imposed time drains? Are you eliminating those?

Chapter 13: Leaning Our Sales Process

Process is a fundamental part of "Lean." We can't possibly be Lean without process. The process provides a framework to ensure we are executing consistently, effectively, and efficiently. It enables us to measure results. It provides a basis to analyze what we do and constantly improve.

If we are taking a random walk to accomplish an outcome, we can't identify those parts of the walk that create value, those parts that are waste, or how to achieve our outcome in the most effective and efficient manner possible. Without a process, achievement of a goal, perhaps winning a deal is pure chance. Consistently achieving a goal, our quotas, or personal earning goals, is anyone's guess.

High performance sales people leave nothing to chance. They select and pursue opportunities that maximize their ability to win. They structure their approach to the territory to consistently achieve their goals (usually their personal goals are higher than their quotas).

So if you don't believe in a "sales process," don't waste your time reading this chapter. Also recognize you will always be outperformed, but we need people like you, because by comparison it further differentiates high performers.

Now that I've gotten that off my chest, how do we "Lean" our sales process?

As you may recall from earlier chapters, the cornerstone of Lean thinking is about value. Every step, every activity is about creating value. Steps and activities that don't create value are waste. Waste detracts from value; it creates cost for our customers, our companies, ourselves.

Too often our sales processes don't work or aren't effective because we have created them based on the things we want to do and when we want to do them, but they may have little to do with the things that create value. Consequently, there is a lot of misdirected or low impact effort. I think there are a number of simple steps we might consider to "Lean our sales process." I will cover a few here.

Our sales process is not aligned with our customers' buying processes. Despite the hundreds of white papers on this, too many sales processes have been built from the inside out. The focus on what we want to do, not how our customers are buying and how we align our activities with the way they buy. There are some that might argue the ultimate in "Leaning the sales process" is to totally eliminate it and focus only on the customer buying process. It's a fair argument, but the major flaw in the argument is there are things that sales people have to do through the selling process that are and will always be totally independent of the customer buying process. Two quick examples are:

   1. Is the customer in our sweet spot?

2. Aligning our resources to create and deliver a solution to the customer.

In the first, the customer doesn't care whether they are in our sweet spot; they don't even know what a sweet spot is. But clearly, if we don't focus on customers in our sweet spot, then we are wasting our time and theirs. In the latter case, in building a solution to respond to what the customer is trying to achieve, we have activities that are independent of the customer.

They create value for the customer, but they don't directly involve the customer. So there need be a buying process owned by the customer and a selling process owned by us. Both need be aligned and where possible integrated.

Our sales process hasn't changed in X years. Often I encounter this situation. I go into a company, I start to talk to the sales people, "Does your company have a sales process, and do you use it?" Too often, the answers are, "Yes and Not at all, it's useless." Sales people don't typically reject things that help them close more deals more quickly. So when I see them not using a sales process I typically find it's old and irrelevant or just poorly designed and irrelevant. How our customer buy is changing. What and how we sell is changing. We must constantly update and refine our sales process.

We have used the default sales process that came with our CRM system, or the default process that our Sales Training Company used. So we are going to use the same process that 1000's of others are using; regardless of what they sell and to who? How can that possibly be an efficient effective process that is aligned with our sweet spot; those customers where we create the greatest value? These generic processes can't possibly align with our customers' buying processes. Our sales process is unique to us. It must be aligned with our corporate strategies and priorities, it must be aligned with how we create the greatest value for our customers, it must be aligned with our customers buy. The default processes in our CRM systems or provided by Sales Training Companies are nothing more than place holders. Since they are not unique to us, inevitably there are a lot of missing steps or irrelevant steps both of which create wasted effort and diminish the value we create for our customers. It is incumbent on us to replace those placeholders with OUR Process. It is not the fault of the CRM or Sales Training providers though it's critical that they tell you; you need to replace their default processes and they can create great value for you by helping you do that.

Our sales process does not clearly identify our sweet spot or force us to disqualify any opportunities that are outside our sweet spot. Our sweet spot is the set of customers where we create our greatest value both in what we sell and how we support our customers' ability to buy. It takes great insight, understanding, and discipline to know your sweet spot. Too often, organizations don't do this. Their targeting process is "if they fog a mirror and have money, they are a prospect." Leaning our sales process requires great clarity about who our customer is and what value we create for those customers. Investing time outside these is waste.

Our sales process has been over-engineered. This may seem to be in conflict with "Lean," but actually isn't. Typically when we think of lean in manufacturing terms, we think of very precise steps and flow, with zero ambiguity or variance. We may be able to define every possible outcome to a manufacturing flow and define the steps in handling these. There are large elements of the sales process which involve great creativity, adaptability, and nimbleness. Lean can be very powerful in these environments not by being overly prescriptive, but by providing us a framework in which we can assess each action, asking, "Does this create value in helping the customer and I reach our shared goal?" If the answer is positive, then our activities are not waste. If the answer is negative, then the activity is waste and should be eliminated. This is probably one of the most difficult concepts to grasp in thinking about applying Lean to selling and to sales processes. But, too often, I see organization thinking they are applying a strong process discipline by trying to define every single step, every single outcome, every single next step for each of those outcomes, and so on. I have literally seen flow charts that cover an entire wall, that try to anticipate everything that might come up in a sales situation. They become impossible for the sales person to execute and slow our customers down. When I encounter these situations, I sometimes imagine the sales person saying to the customer, "I am sorry, I can't skip to step G of your buying process because my process requires me to do C, D, E, F first."

Our sales people don't have the ability to evaluate and adapt what they do to maximize the value they create. This is somewhat related to the previous point. Sales and the selling process is partially a scientific, disciplined approach that is repeatable. At the same time, Sales and the selling process is a creative endeavour. Each customer is different; their needs change as we progress through their process, and how we engage them changes as we help them reach the outcome of making a decision. Lean when applied to creative processes needs to provide the sales person with the framework by which the sales person can evaluate each activity for the value created. In some cases we will skip steps in the sales process because they do not create value (based on a decision we make, not sloppiness). Sometimes we have to reorder the steps, sometimes we have to add new steps each to address the specific situation. Making sure sales people understand Lean principles, giving them the tools by which to evaluate everything they do, eliminating those steps that do not create value, eliminating everything that creates waste is critical to maximizing the performance of our people and teams. This is probably the most difficult aspect of applying Lean principles to sales and the sales process, but it is, perhaps, the most powerful thing we can do in driving the highest levels of performance in our organizations.

I know there is more, but I will stop here.

Chapter 14: High Variability Low Productivity

Sales people don't like the routine! We do different things every day. Each situation is different, each call is different. There is huge variability in our jobs or so we like to think. But is it really true? Is it really true that we can't plan our days, that there aren't some standard practices or processes that we leverage?

The job of the sales person is certainly not routine. Each sales situation is different, each customer situation is different all this is true. But it's important to understand the difference between the "content" of what we do and the structure of what we do. If everything were truly different, we would be incredibly unproductive. Our win rates would plummet, our sales cycles would be endless, and our ability to achieve our goals would be completely out of our control.

Our jobs aren't as unpredictable as we like to think or the excuses we tend to make. Think about it......

The cornerstone to high performance sales is the Sales Process. The sales process is the set of activities and steps we undertake that most effectively and efficiently enable us to engage with the customer moving them through their buying process and helping them reach a decision. The sales process is based on our best experience in selling. It is the set of activities that we know consistently enable us to win. Without a sales process, we are just wandering aimlessly.

The next element to reducing the variability in what we do is Sales Call Planning. Not planning our meetings is a waste of our time, but more importantly, our customers'! Planning our calls assures that both you and your customers are prepared to accomplish something in the meeting, that we create value for each other and that we are moving through our selling and buying processes.

We also do Account and Territory Planning or we should. How do we expand our relationships in the account or territory? How do we maximize the business we get from each, growing our share and relationships? The most effective sales people don't just do this randomly, but they have a structured process; they analyze their accounts and territories, assessing the potential. They conduct structured marketing and prospecting programs. They build and nurture relationships over time.

Finally, putting structure to our days and weeks is important to maximizing our effectiveness. Blocking time, prospecting, customer meetings, preparation, learning, research all enable us to accomplish things and move to accomplishing our goals.

High variability destroys productivity and effectiveness. If we insist on high variability in the way we do our jobs, it's like living in Bill Murray's "Ground Hog Day" all the time. We end up being very busy but accomplishing very little.

Don't succumb to the excuse of not putting structure and process to the way you (and your organization) operate. If you want to maximize your impact, win rate, results and effectiveness, examine every aspect of how you work. Examine everything you do; sure the content discussions in each meeting you have will vary (not as much as we think), but you know the basic structures and processes that drive your effectiveness. Strive to reduce the variability to maximize your productivity.

Chapter 15: Making Lean Six Sigma Work in Sales

Numerous businesses have had successful experiences implementing Lean Six Sigma in sales. The success stories offer proof that the methodology works, as well as providing some best practice guidelines for implementing Lean Six Sigma in sales.

For a number of years, businesses in a wide range of industries have been successfully implementing Lean and Six Sigma in manufacturing and engineering, and more recently in the transactional processes in finance, administration and customer service. The last business area to see this improvement methodology arrive was the sales department. But already it is proving its value there too.

Numerous businesses have had success implementing Lean Six Sigma in sales and achieving the breakthrough benefits that have become commonplace in other organizational functions and processes. The success stories from industry leaders and innovators offer proof that the methodology works, as well as providing some best practice guidelines for implementing Lean Six Sigma in sales.

Selecting the Right Project Focus Area

A common question for organizations considering the extension of Lean Six Sigma into sales is: "What types of projects are best for applying Lean Six Sigma in sales?" Based on experience as well as the best practices of companies such as GE, Johnson & Johnson, Honeywell, Motorola and others, six types of projects represent fertile ground for early projects:

1. Lead generation.
2. Sales proposal process.
3. Sales forecasting.
4. New product launch.
5. Sales force efficiency and effectiveness.
6. Voice of the customer.

The six project areas can be roughly grouped into two categories. Category 1 consists of the first four project areas. These projects focus primarily on the improvement of sub-processes that are related to or supportive of field sales. Companies often find it helpful to start with a Category 1 project for a number of reasons. First, the processes involved in Category 1 projects are relatively easy to identify, visualize and map. In addition, data and metrics on process performance are relatively easy to collect and define. The processes involved are usually repeatable in a fairly consistent manner. And finally, solutions and improvements are easier to identify and implement than in Category 2 projects.

Category 1 projects, however, do not directly increased sales. Instead, these projects primarily create improvements in the efficiency of internal processes. For example, generating better qualified leads and speeding the flow of proposals to customers will undoubtedly lead to more revenue. Likewise, improved reliability of sales forecasts will impact the availability of products, which will ultimately impact revenue as well. However, the gains from Category 1 projects will not, by themselves, generate the breakthrough results that have become the hallmark of Lean Six Sigma initiatives.

It is the Category 2 project areas "sales force efficiency and effectiveness" and "voice of the customer" that generate the breakthrough results. These projects are far more complex and challenging in terms of identifying consistent processes, collecting reliable quantitative data, identifying root causes, and finding and implementing solutions. Nevertheless, because Category 2 projects impact the field sales force and selling processes directly, they create solutions and improvements that drive significant and sustainable revenue and margin growth.

Sales Force Efficiency and Effectiveness Projects

Companies with a sales force that calls on many customers and represent fairly standard products and services are the best candidates for sales force efficiency and effectiveness (SFE&E) projects. These companies are in such industries as pharmaceutical, medical devices and hospital products, financial services, and information technology. Although sales representatives working for these companies all have more or less the same market and customer opportunities in terms of local territories, products to sell, competition, etc., there is typically significant variation in the performance and results of individual representatives. In Six Sigma terminology, a significant amount of process variation exists which,

83

if eliminated, will yield breakthrough improvement in output; in this case revenue growth.

In SFE&E projects, standard Six Sigma tools such as fishbone diagrams and the 5 Whys are used to identify the root causes of variation in performance and results of different sales. Soft (and difficult-to-measure) factors, such as selling behaviours and skills, are frequently more significant root causes than are hard factors such as job experience. Nevertheless, even soft factors can be addressed effectively. For example, best practice selling behaviours and tactics can be identified and replicated across the sales force, and coaching by sales managers can be applied to reinforce best practices and enable the development of best-in-class selling behaviours. Often, simply measuring and communicating publicly the performance of different sales representatives' results in sales growth. This is no doubt due to the competitive nature of salespeople.

Voice of the Customer Projects

Voice of the Customer (VOC) projects are most attractive for companies with a concentrated market and customer segment. These companies operate in such industries as aerospace, automotive and household appliances and have a smaller, highly consultative sales force, typically organized around a few key accounts.

VOC projects are targeted on driving customer share or market penetration by first identifying each individual customer's "basic requirements." Basic requirements are those measurable standards of product, service and relationship quality that a supplier must meet in order to remain a supplier to an account. Of course, meeting basic requirements is not enough to ensure continued sales and customer share growth, especially since competitors within the same account are likewise trying to grow customer share. In order to achieve competitive differentiation, companies must learn what really pleases the customer, and finally what it takes to "delight" the customer. Delight, in this case, means pleasing customers beyond the customers' own expectations.

In a typical VOC project, Six Sigma tools are applied to identify basic requirements, what pleases customers and what is likely to delight them. Root causes or opportunities can then be identified that, when addressed, will enable the supplier to not only meet the customer's basic requirements 100 percent of the time, but also will lead to the discovery of delight factors. Implementing improvements and solutions that address delight factors is ultimately what will lead to breakthrough revenue growth.

Some Common Keys to Success

The selection of the best project or projects to implement in order to bring Lean Six Sigma to sales depends on a number of factors, which are different for every company. However it is important to keep in mind a few things that are key to the success of any implementation.

1. Lean Six Sigma in sales projects must focus on increasing profitability by driving the top

line of the business (revenue), more than just driving down expenses. As revenues increase, the productivity and cost-to-revenue ratios of the sales force will improve by definition. However, salespeople will avoid, and even resist, anything that they see as an attempt solely to squeeze costs out of the sales force. On the other hand, they will embrace anything that they believe will help them make more sales.

2. Involving the field sales force directly in projects is essential, but it should not require pulling people out of the field for extended training sessions and project team meetings. Typically, salespeople can work virtually and remain in the field while still participating in a project. Training in the Lean Six Sigma tools and methods can be done on a "just-in-time" basis and teams can be supported by Black Belts, even if the Black Belts have only limited experience in sales.

3. And, as is usually the case with organizational change initiatives, keep it simple. Most implementations require use of a handful of key tools data collection plans, fishbone diagrams, Pareto charts, 5 whys, and a few others which can be easily adapted for the sales environment.

One final thought: Do it now! Keep in mind that while a company is debating whether or not to bring the powerful Lean Six Sigma methodology to its sales staff, competitors may already be using it.

Chapter 16: Marketing Needs Six Sigma Methodology to Improve

Marketing needs to do a better job of using statistics and especially variation. When I start talking numbers to people, and what they mean, I get looked at like someone that is just trying to complicate a creative process. Improvement is about numbers. Measurement is about numbers. The truth is, marketing is about numbers. So why not employ more of the Six Sigma methodology? I understand that achieving the quality that Six Sigma represents may be difficult but the principles and tools should, nevertheless be utilized.

Your present marketing data is more than likely flawed and ineffective. Comparing one number to another is just ineffective. Comparison is limited because numbers are subject to variation and without variation taken into account the data is distorted.

Comparing numbers to specifications will not lead to improvement. Specifications are the Voice of the Customer. The specification approach will not reveal insights into how the process works and as a result will not tell you where you are, how you got there and how or what to improve to get out of it.

Voice of the Customer defines what you want. Voice of the Process defines what you will get from the system. Management job is to bring Voice of Customer in alignment with Voice of the Process.

Can you start using proper data in your marketing process? We recommends starting tomorrow by:
1. Begin to collect the right data.
2. Insist upon interpreting within their context.
3. Filter out the noise before considering any value as a potential signal.
4. Cease to ask for explanations of noise.
5. Understand that no matter how the results may stack up against the specifications, a process which displays statistical control is performing as consistently as possible.
6. Always distinguish between Voice of Custom and Voice of Process.
7. Help others take action on assignable causes.

I typically find that most companies are not ready to start a Six Sigma project because of the lack of measurement in their processes. Having the working knowledge of Black Belt can greatly enhance getting started down the path. It is a journey and depending upon the scope of the project, not one to hastily jump into.

Chapter 17: Kanban in Marketing

Kanban is any signalling device that gives authorization for a supplying process to know what to produce, or for a material handler to know what items to replenish. For example: a physical paper card placed in a container of parts. When stored items are actually used, the Kanban card gets "freed" (perhaps it was in the bottom of the container), and gets put back into a Kanban stand where the Kanban "requests" are fulfilled.

Kanban

Kanban is a way of limiting work in process (WIP) and the amount of new work that is introduced into the process. As a result, work would be pulled from the previous stage as work is completed and levels demand. It emphasizes throughput rather than numbers. In other chapters in this book, you would recognize the emphasis I put on throughput and the need for this to be monitored in the sales and marketing process.

The Reasons for a Kanban

1. **Improve your Marketing Cycle, Increase your Revenue:** Speed is important in the buying process. Your total cycle time can be improved. However, it seldom can be done without more feedback loops in your system.

Develop process blitzes to reduce these non-value times. Go to Gemba or the customer's place of work and find out what happens during this time. See what is stopping them from moving forward. It may be an internal constraint within their company. However, the constraint may be yours. You may not be responding to the customer's latest needs. Your ability to focus your resources on the customer needs may provide the overall clarity he needs to make a more rapid decision.

2. **Improve throughput, cut your customers in half:** In a manufacturing system cutting WIP just about always will increase throughput. Why? You end up working only on what is needed and when it is needed. You also will have less waste, less material to handle and fewer mistakes. Good things happen when you are not handling excessive amount of material. In a marketing system cutting the amount of customers in half works very much the same way. You end up working on what a customer truly needs and want. Your marketing will become more personal, more direct, and fewer mistakes.

3. **Using the Six Sigma Tollgate in your Marketing Funnel:** Have you thought of using DMAIC as a way of defining your marketing funnel? We looked at Define, Measure, Analyze, Improve and Control and utilized these basic principles to walk a customer through the marketing funnel. In

other chapters of this book, I discussed the ability to create a shorter cycle time by decreasing the non-value time in between each of these stages. One of the methods of doing this is to have a strong call to action for a prospect to move from one stage to the next. However, how do you know if a customer is ready to move from one stage to the next?

4. **What kind of questions would you ask at a tollgate?** Later in this book I go through the concept of using a tollgate in your marketing funnel. Below is a list of questions that might help generate a few ideas that you may want to consider.

The essential points needed in a Kanban system are:
1. Stock points
2. Replenishment Signal
3. Quick Feedback
4. Frequent Replenishment

DMAIC Marketing

If you would consider the typical marketing cycle as a prospect moves from one stage to another, you imagine it as step by step process and certain events taking place within that stage. With a Kanban method or a tollgate you could have certain trigger points for each stage or even a phase within that stage allowing one marketing effort to pull from the previous. The method would also limit the number of prospects within that cycle so that the proper amount could be managed or more importantly satisfied! Or, you could have an unlimited supply of leads flowing into each stage? You probably wish you had the latter.

Chapter 18: Six Sigma Tollgate in Your Marketing Funnel

Later in this book I will go through the process of using DMAIC as a way of defining your marketing funnel. We will look at Define, Measure, Analyze, Improve and Control and utilized these basic principles to walk a customer through the marketing funnel. In other chapters, I discussed the ability to create a shorter cycle time by decreasing the non-value time in between each of these stages. One of the methods of doing this is to have a strong call to action for a prospect to move from one stage to the next. However, how do you know if a customer is ready to move from one stage to the next?

A lesson that marketers can learn from the Six Sigma Methodology is the utilization of the Tollgate. The tollgate is use to clearly define measurable objectives that will allow a prospect to pass through the gate or to the next stage, or be held until the objectives are completed. Consider how many times that a prospect enters another stage of your marketing funnel and has not experienced the previous stages. When this happens, do you find yourself explaining at the last moment certain objections that should have been dealt with previously? The tendency to slip into the next phase can be common early in the timeline. The desire to move someone quickly through the funnel and to the buy stage or the "close" will often compromise your original standards set. Our typical response is to flood the prospect with the additional information, or make additional sales calls to explain the situation. More than likely this situation will cause the process to be held and dealt with as a "special" situation. Other times, a tollgate is created on an as needed bases causing further confusion downstream.

Overview of a Tollgate

Tollgate Reviews help determine whether all the goals within each stage have been achieved successfully and whether the project can progress to the next stage.

Preparing for a successful Tollgate Review

Many reviews fail due to lack of preparation. If you are going to have a tollgate review, prepare for it. This should include a minimum of a check sheet, milestone list, deliverable documents, etc. for review. This could even be an automated process that the customer knowingly or even unknowingly completes.

Let the numbers be your guide. Spend time developing good metrics and methodologies for their capture. If you do Tollgate review process is as simple as you either made the numbers or you did not. If you leave metrics be general like using the words most in lieu of a defined number, you will create an ineffective tollgate. If you always find exceptions to allow someone to pass through the gate defeats the purpose of the tollgate. Stopping the line, will take some courage initially and that is why many times management or an independent party, in Six Sigma it is the Black Belt, must press the button.

A Tollgate is exactly what it sounds like. The gate comes down and you must pay the toll before continuing. Now, what makes this such a strong feature is how many times do you ever pay the toll without knowing where you are going?

Chapter 19: Improved Marketing Cycle Leads to Increased Revenue

The very best thing about organizing and "systemizing" your marketing is that you now have more tools at your disposal to understand and facilitate but not manipulate your customer's efforts. A Value Stream Map is quite useful in visualizing and providing calculations for cycle time.

Before I go into the explanation, the question should probably be. Who Cares? Throughput or decreasing your Marketing Cycle time can have very beneficial results. If you put customers through the cycle quicker it will more than likely increase revenue. If it takes one person 60 days in a normal cycle time, and you reduce it to 30, you should be able to double sales for any given period. It may also reduce expenses as there would be less people in the cycle at any given period. So increasing throughput can be accepted as a good thing.

I am not going to be so naive and say that you can remove all the non-value added time and close a sale in less number of days. The point that I am delivering is that; you must learn how to manage the non-value time more effectively. Most companies deliver good presentations, advertise and get good PR. Where they fall short is handing the baton from one stage to the next. Non-activity turns marketing rotten. Even with good (refrigeration) techniques our leads may go stone cold.

Marketing Cycle

If you can make an effort to understand the customer's process during this time, significant gains may be made. Your actual processing time is insignificant in most marketing. It is the lead time between the processes that are important. Consider, for example, if we would increase the offer to move someone from the Trust stage to the Trial Stage. Reducing the time from 5 days to 2 days or not at all. Or maybe, you have noticed that quicker conversions happen when they attend a webinar. What would happen if we paid them to come to the Webinar? You may find out segmenting your process halfway through the cycle would allow customers to better understand the results that they may gain from your product. Many of your features and benefits may be confusing to certain prospects that are not utilizing those particular features anyway.

Speed is important in the buying process. Your total cycle time can be improved. However, it seldom can be done without more feedback loops in your system. Develop process blitzes to reduce these non-value times. Go to Gemba or the customer's place of work and find out what happens during this time. See what is stopping them from moving forward. It may be an internal constraint within their company. However, the constraint may be yours. You may find your responses lack clarity. You may not be responding to the customer's latest needs. Your ability to focus your resources on the customer needs may provide the overall clarity he needs this to make a more rapid decision.

One method is to create a vision of shorter cycle time, greater segmentation of your customers. It will enable you to do fewer actions in the cycle and much quicker. "It is not the big that ate the small. It is the fast that eat the slow" Cycle times need to be addresses and improved.

Chapter 20: Speed May Be the Biggest Determent to Your Marketing Success

The company that gets to the customer first, the company that releases the product first, the company that slides in and closes the sale while you are still waiting to get the final specifications, all demonstrate how important speed is to your marketing success.

Speed is much, much more than the ability to run your customer through your marketing cycle. It is an integral part of building a marketing system that responds to customer's needs. Having built in trigger points to help you identify your customer's readiness to proceed to the next stage in your Marketing Hourglass is imperative.

I discussed handing the baton off in an earlier chapter and how many times that gets dropped from one stage to the next. It is similar to an athlete starting the season off and building his "speed" back up. Or a student taking the same test after summer break and scoring lower. These things happen because of the lack of activity during the non-value added time that you have identified in your Value Stream Mapping Process. The lack of speed in your marketing process equates to the lack of engagement that you have with your customer. This can be one of the most effective uses of social media and a good content marketing strategy. The engagement of your customer is driven by the needs they identify with your product.

Here are some examples of items that may help in decreasing that non-value added time.

1. Attempting too late or too early to move a customer to the next stage.

2. Not building upon the previous stage by starting with different content. You effectively lose the momentum that was built by the earlier stage.

3. Reinforce the previous stage. Creating the linkages between stages is extremely important. It is a great time for a warm-up.

4. Make sure the customer is on the right airplane. You have been there, even if it is embarrassing when the stewardess says this plane is headed to England, and you are not going there; you are getting off. If a customer is not ready for this stage give him a graceful exit and provide them an opportunity to get off, or you may lose him forever.

5. Make a better offer. Each stage should create a better offer than the previous. You have a more qualified customer at this stage so treat them that way.

6. Create interactive platforms or trials that the customer can use or interact with to solve some of their problems. This happens quite frequently in the construction business when someone leases a bulldozer to a contractor or online with free down-loadable software.

7. A superior call to action, an offer that cannot be refused to go the next stage.

Even with these improvements, without a marketing system in place to monitor results and improve upon them, you will fall behind. Speed is not automation. Automation can be a component of developing speed but don't mistake the use of automation. People even in the online society we have created still want conversation and personal connection surrounding the product. Especially, in regards to a service they may purchase. They want a live body behind the curtain or in our case the Marketing Hourglass.

Chapter 21: DMAIC Funnel

If you search Google, there are thousands of images for the marketing funnel depicted. All having a little different twist. All of them depicting a systematic way to go from initial contact to buy and many of them adding the referral and repeat stages. I believe a systematic way to manage your marketing should not be an option but a fundamental of marketing. However, with this many options can there be a system?

We think of segmentation both in a horizontal fashion and a vertical. Horizontal will typically result in segments such as: Direct, Internet, Distributor, Joint-Venture and so on. This funnel allows you to assign different products to each process stage in the hope of maximizing efforts.

However, if you attempt to improve your Marketing Funnel, how would you go about it? Being a Lean Six Sigma Black Belt, the Marketing Funnel bears a close resemblance to the DMAIC process of Six Sigma. Not that I am trying to replace the marketing funnel with DMAIC, but it certainly would not hurt to analyze the resemblance to improve our marketing process. And if you know anything about Lean Six Sigma, the one thing we will attack is variation. However, just using some generic definitions of DMAIC and relating them to the Marketing Funnel can create some interesting observations.

1. Define

Purpose: Identify the clients, their needs and requirements. **Deliverable:** State the need of the client and the problem.

2. Measure

Purpose: Quantify Process Performance.
Deliverable: Determine baseline process performance.

3. Analyze

Purpose: Identify, Verify and Quantify Root causes.
Deliverable: Statistically linking input with output.

4. Improve

Purpose: Create the Solution and Validate.
Deliverable: Optimizing Process Operating Conditions.

5. Control

Purpose: Document and Standardize Process.
Deliverable: Meet Critical to Quality (CTQ) consistently (Involvement)

Looking at your Marketing Funnel from the DMAIC viewpoint is not that far-fetched, is it?

1. Define Stage

Six Sigma or Lean practitioners would view what I say about DMAIC as hardly revolutionary. Marketers may view it as just a way for a Black Belt to find a way to manoeuvre themselves into some of their market share. I happen to be more of a marketing guy, than a

106

Lean or Six Sigma technician. But I believe that Marketing should be a process and when viewed that way, many of the principles and tools of Lean and Six Sigma start making a lot of sense.

Marketing people view their role as a series of events, task and campaigns versus a process. Not to over simplify but a calendar is a static document and does not support the use of a process. Once you start systematizing or building a marketing process deliverables, stability, variation and measurable results become important. Hence, Lean or Six Sigma can be a significant partner in improving the Marketing process.

Use of the DMAIC process is usually reserved for solving problem with existing processes. Other methodologies, such as DMEDI are used in the design functions and may be more suitable for certain marketing campaigns. In this chapter, I am going to concentrate on the DMAIC method.

My early chapters correlated the Marketing Funnel to DMAIC and how we may use that methodology to walk our customer through our marketing process. The first stage in the DMAIC Methodology is the Define stage. In the marketing funnel the opening stage is usually reserved for the awareness stage. We typically think of this as our lead generation efforts of getting someone to enter our funnel. Even though we may use efforts as permissions style marketing it is still very much a bait and switch tactic. If we truly believe the Inbound Marketing is what is necessary in today's marketing, using the Six Sigma Define stage opens a more correct way of entry into the funnel.

My explanation of the Define Stage previously

Purpose: Identify the clients, their needs and requirements.
Deliverable: State the need of the client and the problem

Expanding on this explanation the Define stage typically asks us to start with a problem statement. In the marketing sense, can you define the problem that you solve for your customers clearly? Where the problem statement describes the pain, the next statement should describe the relief that is to be expected. After that, we go into a process that is typically defined as Voice of the Customer. There are typically two major categories that are required; Output requirements and Service Requirements. The output requirements relate to the final product or service that is delivered to the customer. The service requirements relate to how the customer would like to be treated and served during the process. The final step in the Define stage is to document the process. Typically, this is done with a high level process map. Don't worry about it being completely correct as we will use it and develop it further in the remaining processes.

Six Sigma has some great tools on how to obtain and measure these processes such as Kano Analysis, Process Map and SIPOC. I just wonder why marketers shy away from them.

2. Measure Stage

Processes lend themselves to measurement. If you treat your marketing as a process, then you should be able to measure your marketing. The define stage answers the question. What is important? The measure stage will answer that question by asking. How are we doing?

The purpose of the Measure stage is to quantify process performance and deliverable and to determine baseline process performance. Without these facts, you will be very ineffective in improving performance. This is the stage which is most difficult for the novice. Adequate measurements in the current state are simply not there many times and as a result we either never get out of this stage by trying to be too precise or we move on without inadequate information that causes us to reduce effectiveness of the latter stages. Another common fault is that we start analyzing the data which is the next stage of the process.

Remember that this is a current state not a future state step in the process. Remember, if you think something that you are doing is not measurable, there is someone already measuring it, YOUR CUSTOMER. This brings us back to the marketing funnel and I am correlating the measure phase to the consider phase. In the consider phase, or the like stage of the funnel, prospects are aware of you but now you must prepare them to consider you as a worthy candidate. How do you do that? In the DMAIC methodology we use tools such as Critical to

Quality and other tools to determine what is important to a prospect. Instead of thinking about this step from an internal point of view step back and consider what the prospect would use to measure your product or service and make the decision to move through the funnel. Developing measures with customer input will certainly help a prospect move though the funnel.

At this stage, do you know how a prospect is measuring you? What is the most Critical to quality standard that influences your product or service? What is more critical than others? The old saying is that people perform by how they are measured? If your company is based on how they are being measured do you have measurements in places that you are performing too?

This is an area that we taking the process map to a deeper level or developing the current state in a Value Stream Mapping process.

Customers' expectations have three aspects:
1. Assume
2. Expected
3. Desired.

The assumed customer requirements are the basics and typically are only communicated when the customer is dissatisfied. The expected customers have come to anticipate, certain features from their experience or by observing them in the marketplace. The desired customer requirements, however, are not objectively communicated to the supplier. They represent what desires the customer would really like to have met but does not expect. Some call these customer delights. Could you be scaling yourself in these three areas?

Developing marketing measurements requires a mind-set for accountability. Measurements must be understandable, quantifiable, and economic. Customers objectively and clearly state these requirements and pay the supplier for meeting their explicit expectations. We must be there listening and responding to them. The more these requirements are met, the more the customer is satisfied.

3. Analyze Stage

The first 2-steps of the DMAIC process answered the questions. What is important and how are we doing? We also considered the marketing funnel stages of Awareness and Consider. The third stage of the process in DMAIC is Analyze and in the Marketing funnel it is Prefer or Trust. Analyzing is about finding ROOT CAUSE to the already described process steps of Define and Measure.

This is also time to reiterate that the thinking process must be about the external prospect or customer. Are listening to your prospects requirements and measuring yourself on how you are performing based on those requirements? Have you properly identified, verified and quantified the root causes of their pain and statistically linked input with output? If this seems mind boggling, you are at the proper stage. Now, is the time to make sense of all the data and confirm the validity of it? However, this is the time that so-called common sense can get in the way. Even at the most basic level of Six Sigma training, examples are given of problems that when reviewed, the data seems to point at an obvious answer. It is an eye-opening experience when you input the data into a statistical program such as Mini-tab and see the results. If you would not have analyzed the problem correctly, you may have been working on a problem that did not exist and as a result have little impact. Remember the old adage, numbers do not lie! However, garbage in will equal garbage out, verification of the data is extremely important.

Using a high level process map or as I prefer, a Value Stream Map is important. The visualization of the process will help as you analyze the data. The first several times you do this, it may only involve several simple tools such as a Fishbone Diagram and/or a Pareto Chart. This is also the stage we look at Value-Added activities. We can very often find many things that are adding little value from the prospects point of view at this time. Sometimes significant reductions that will pay for the entire improvement policy can be found in this stage.

As a prospect, I may have entered your funnel with a specific problem and now determined that you are someone that I should consider. It is time for me to analyze your organization and start developing preferences. How does marketing react to this role? Marketing at this time needs to identify root cause. I believe that it is very difficult for a prospect to move from consider to prefer without having their root cause addressed. If you start with the definition of the problem you are solving and take a marketing segment or even an individual prospect and using a tool such as the fishbone diagram, you will be able to determine whether your product or service addresses root cause. If it does not, is there a reason to continue with this customer? Is it a good fit? Maybe, there is a better product or service you should be offering?

Definitions of Preferred Process Maps:

The Fishbone Diagram, also known as the Cause and Effect Diagram or Ishikawa Diagram, is a graphical construct used to identify and explore on a single chart, in increasing detail commonly using the 5 Why technique, the possible causes which lead to a given effect. The ultimate aim is to work down through the causes to identify basic root causes of a problem.

A Pareto chart, named after Vilfredo Pareto, is a type of chart which contains both bars and a line graph. The bars display the values in descending order, and the line graph shows the cumulative totals of each category, left to right. The purpose of the Pareto chart is to highlight the most important among a (typically large) set of factors. In quality control, it often represents the most common sources of defects, the highest occurring type of defect, or the most frequent reasons for customer complaints, and so on.

4. Improve Stage

The first 3 steps of the DMAIC process answered the questions. What is important, how are we doing and what is wrong? We also considered the marketing funnel stages of Awareness, Consider and prefer. The fourth stage of the process in DMAIC is Improve and in the Marketing funnel it is Evaluate or Trust. Now, we get to the stage that we have been waiting for, create the solution, validate and optimize the process. Or, in simpler terms, what needs to be done?

After all the hard work of the previous stages, it goes without saying you must work on addressing the root cause of the problem not something else. It sounds silly to say, but the people that were good at doing all the detective work in the previous two steps are not necessarily the problem solvers in the organization. Roles may shift and different agendas may creep into this stage. This is important if this shift takes place, stay on task and work on the root cause.

All solutions are not equal. Typically, without too much analysis you can weed through them and narrow the good ones down to several ones that address the root cause. The remaining ones should be systematically eliminated or ranked in order of feasibility to include perceived effectiveness, ease of implementation, within budget constraints, and the ability to measure. What good is a solution if it cannot be measured on how effective it is? Another criterion that I recommend is the ability to pilot test. A sampling of your solution can be a very effective way of deciding between two seemingly equal solutions.

Especially, if one requires a substantial investment. A solution matrix is a very simple and visual tool for comparison. Several other tools that can be used are Tree Diagrams and Design of Experiments (DOE).

This is also the stage that I develop a future state map using the Value Stream Mapping Tool.

Marketers frequently at this stage get someone to evaluate or try the product. They are thinking download for thirty days, use this sample, attend this webinar and other ways of evaluation. My thinking is that after you have accomplished the other three stages of the funnel; you are ready to demonstrate that you solve ROOT CAUSE. Can you? Most jobs are lost at this stage because of a lack of clarity. Your solution must be crystal clear and be without a question on how you will solve the prospects' problem and deliver that solution. It is also imperative that you turn your solution into dollars. What is the ROI you are contributing?

5. Control Stage

The first 4 steps of the DMAIC process answered the questions. What is important, how are we doing, what is wrong and what needs to be done? We also considered the marketing funnel stages of Awareness, consider, prefer and evaluate. The fifth stage of the process in DMAIC is Control and in the Marketing funnel it is the commit or buy stage. This is where in Six Sigma we document the process and standardize meeting critical to quality (CTQ) issues.

This step involves taking the improvements and implementing them. We will document standard operating procedures, create process control plans, and establish a control process. The one final step in handing over the process or transitioning the process for implementation. However, it is imperative that we create an operation that is stable, predictable and meets the customer requirements. The implementation should be supported by documentation and project management to put all the work into practice. Another way of saying this is how are we going to guarantee performance.

In the marketing funnel it comes down to the basic decision to commit or buy the product or service. Clarity is the number one issue that may prevent you from succeeding if your product/service meets the criteria for the root cause. Remember, customers want consistency. At this stage, you will see price and the confidence that you can deliver what you say becoming the greatest issues. If you believe price is the overwhelming issue, just think of how many times you have lost a job to a better known brand. Why? Security and your lack of ability to address the root cause with unquestionable clarity.

Remote control unit The Control process of Six Sigma can certainly teach us a few things. Creating an operation that delivers a stable and predictable outcome is the purpose of not only the Control stage but the entire DMAIC process. If you have identified predictable measures that the customer can visualize and satisfy the root cause of his problem, you are well on your way of obtaining commitment.

Another stage of Control is handing off of the project for implementation. How many marketing projects are not supported by sales or vice versa? Sales efforts can be undermined especially when the process does not provide predictable results. The ability to control this stage of the process may prevent you from caving into unreasonable demands that prospects may place upon you. However, most worries are not about the prospect but in the effort to close sales many organizations will take their eye off the target and take jobs that may or not solve the root cause or problem for the prospect. Seldom in that circumstance will you deliver the product or service that the prospect is hoping for. It may result in over delivering, which not only is wasted but to the prospect unclear and difficult to evaluate appropriately. Sales may look at this and determine that there is a greater degree of flexibility in the product/service than there is and/or that pricing could be adjusted because the next customer may not need all this. This is not a problem of your sales department, rather you having built the platform and handed off a poorly designed control phase. Build a process management plan for implementation and establishing ongoing measure and methods to be used for improvement is crucial to overall success.

Chapter 22: Can Lean Improve Sales?

Clearly, the interest in this issue has been driven by the current global recession. In most cases, the real thrust of the question is whether having lean production and support processes can help a company improve sales. When people respond to this question, most will usually point out that a lean company is highly efficient and that it can offer lower prices and/or faster job turnaround, both of which can help grow sales.

I agree that these attributes of lean can support sales, but lean principles can also be used to improve sales in a more direct way. Marketing and sales is a business process. And because it is a business process, marketing and sales can be analyzed, measured, and improved using process improvement tools such as lean and Six Sigma.

The starting point is to recognize that your marketing and sales process itself must provide value to customers. The objective of the marketing and sales process is to produce customers. To accomplish that objective, the marketing and sales process takes "raw materials" (people or organizations in the marketplace who have the kinds of problems your company can solve) and adds value for them until they are transformed into customers.

How does a marketing and sales process add value to a prospective customer? Primarily by using a range of communications techniques and media to convey information that the prospect needs to make an informed buying decision. So, to begin creating a lean marketing and sales process, draw a map of your existing marketing and sales process. Then look at each activity in your process map and ask yourself some simple questions. Does this activity create value for a prospective customer? If not, it's waste. Then the question becomes. Can the activity be eliminated or substantially reduced? If the activity provides some value, does it provide enough? Is there a way to change the activity so that it will provide more value? Are there "value gaps" in your sales and marketing process? In other words, do your prospective customers need certain information or assistance that your current process is not providing?

Most managers try to solve sales problems by providing training on individual selling skills, or by tweaking the sales compensation program, or by simply demanding more marketing and selling activity; more prospecting, more sales calls, or more quoting. At times, these actions can be useful, but if the underlying marketing and sales process is flawed, or wasteful, or ineffective, they won't solve your sales problem.

Chapter 23: Five Things Sales and Marketing Can Learn from Lean Production

Some companies already know a lot about the transition from traditional to lean production operations. As it turns out, there are remarkable parallels between the lean journey in manufacturing and the lean journey in sales and marketing (sales kaizen).

When implemented effectively, both the benefits and the challenges are remarkably similar:

Prerequisites to Lean in Sales and Marketing

Two key prerequisites are top-down leadership and employee empowerment. They are not mutually exclusive! They are both necessary.

Why?

Because, if everyone agreed what new ways would actually work better, they would be doing it already! It follows that the most important improvements usually involve things some people actively think will not work.

Leadership alone can break through that log-jam by saying, "there is value in learning to manage according to these principles and policies, so go do it."

Good leaders create the environment where healthy, vigorous debates enable employees to try out their ideas while ensuring the organization learns from them.

This is especially true in sales and marketing. Unlike other production environments, where value-add is visible, in sales and marketing value-add is invisible. Sales and marketing has not benefitted from years of measurement and study around how to produce efficiently and effectively.

That is why sales and marketing VPs are generally unable to accomplish much of any process improvement or lean without assistance from outside the company.

Aside from joking about how sales are especially lean these days, corporate managers may be unaware of the mechanisms required for measuring value-add. They need senior management to provide air cover while the pipe is being laid to measure, reduce risks, and create the possibility for real improvement.

Best Practices for Lean in Sales and Marketing

In the lean manufacturing journey, that groundwork and pipe laying involves well-known best practices such as 5S, Value Stream Mapping, Setup Reduction, etc.

Of course, a journey like this requires "soft training," so people understand why the lean journey is required, what concepts are involved, and what their roles will be. It also requires "hard training," about new ways of doing their jobs, and measuring things. Here is a brief rundown of the primary kinds of best-practice projects required for implementing the lean journey in sales and marketing.

1. Sales value stream mapping (alignment)

This is the primary vehicle for enabling the organization to identify how value is created in sales and marketing "production." This enables the team to understand sales production as a system (usually for the first time), so they can prioritize the major elements for improvement.

2. 5S (sort, set in order, shine, standardize, sustain)

5S is more than salespeople cleaning their desks and organizing file cabinets. Sales and process savvy must identify what it takes to do the job, and organize it: examples might include customer value maps, qualification criteria, value propositions, ROI models, and more.

3. Qualification criteria

The first two best-practices enable measuring the quantity of deals flowing through the sales funnel. Qualification criteria enable measuring their quality. A little scientific research in this area explodes myths and tribal knowledge, and shows salespeople how to identify waste and value they can't see on their own.

4. Lead nurturing and lead generation

When salespeople are responsible for doing everything, they inevitably skip some steps, or do them inconsistently. Nothing is more effective for increasing sales flow (pull) than separating lead generation and nurturing from selling itself.

5. Sales Kaizen (PDCA)

Kaizen enabled the Japanese automotive manufacturers to win the automobile wars. Its focus on simple measures and communication is just what the doctors ordered in field sales, where people by nature think independently (and are often geographically dispersed). It also helps management locate the causes of problems so they can improve the system.

Implementing a lean journey in sales and marketing is an immensely profitable journey, once started. It contains all the benefits (and probably more) of its manufacturing counterpart, and the same kinds of challenges as well.

Chapter 24: Driving Lean Process Excellence Success in Sales

A Global Sales Director asks:

What is the top driver of Lean Process Excellence success in sales?

I would say the main driver is the focus on data and evidence from the customer gemba (i.e., field sales activities).

(Since you used "Lean Process Excellence" in the question, I'm going to assume you are familiar with the lingo, so if I use some jargon you are not familiar with please check them out in my book "Lean Handbook".)

Most B2B companies do not have the ability to see what is working or not working in the field with salespeople, which is a key issue. (By the way, it is quite interesting and useful to ask senior executives Why?-Why?-Why? on that, because they typically don't realize how crucial being able to identify what is working or not working in the field really is to the business. This exercise helps them learn that.)

To use process language: Sales Process Excellence requires the customer-facing functions (not just sales) to develop and agree on operating definitions around their "units of production" (terms like "customer," "lead/inquiry," "qualified sales opportunity," etc.) Believe me; they do get highly motivated by this when they realize the company is actually listening!

The reason this drives substantive changes is that it enables management to identify the bottleneck based on data and evidence rather than on gut feel and the opinions of HIPPOs (highest paid persons in the organization). Usually, this new evidence enables them to hypothesize root causes and develop workable countermeasures far more effectively.

For example, one division president's gut emotion told him the "national account managers are a bunch of farmers, and we need hunters instead." A proper kaizen enabled the national account teams to collect VOC, define the stages of the customer journey, and prove with data that most of their time (80 %!) were devoted to chasing down and solving problems with customer orders they already won.

Now, why were they were so intent on farming? Turns out the national accounts were not generated by any kind of intentional sales process, but grew out of the needs of some of the larger customers in the industry. Since the company had grown its business by depending on the distribution channel to handle customer needs and these national accounts were direct business, by definition there was no customer service infrastructure to enable the right combination of products and services to arrive at the right time in the right customer location. Maybe this was not something the senior executive wanted to hear, but it was a reality that needed to be faced for sure! Only after this was solved could the Sales VP and his national account team have a chance at succeeding in finding new national accounts.

Typically, sales process excellence initiatives enable companies to go from unmeasured to measured in crucial performance indicators such as:

1. Visitors to the company's website who find what they are looking for.
2. Channel partner's ability to achieve their business growth objectives with the company.
3. Flow (quantity over time) of prospects and customers through the sales value stream (and ability to identify the bottleneck).
4. Conversion of sales opportunities (quality of leads, opportunities, and deals which dramatically improves accuracy of the sales forecast).
5. Customer satisfaction and/or net promoter scores.

Remember the old story of the blind men and the elephant? One blind man believes an elephant is like a tree trunk, another that it is like a snake, etc. This is exactly what happens when the company president thinks the problem with the sales force is training, while the sales VP thinks it is lead generation, and the Marketing VP thinks it is poor branding. Until you go through the effort to define your terms and make the flow visible, you can't begin to really understand the nature of the complex production system you are dealing with.

Imagine how shocked those old blind men would be if suddenly they could see the smelly, ugly elephant they were dealing with! Sales process excellence is like that. What you see might be scary or wonderful at first. But if your goal is to build a sales dynasty in your industry, you can't do it without first being able to see what you are actually dealing with.

Lean Sales

In sales, there is often a fine line between value creation and waste. An order gained with an excellent profit margin with a strategic customer or an order lost due to a lack of customer context analysis and a poor offer. Sales have the task of generating the PULL that production needs.

Going Gemba in sales means going to the customer. Understanding the world of the customer. This is the starting point for a maximisation of value creation and the realisation of sales potentials. In the analysis in the sales team we recognise patterns of success and develop processes and methods for avoiding waste and increasing efficiency.

Whether it is in the definition of target customers, analysis of enquiries, presentation of offers or gaining of orders; the aim is to build up a reliably effective, efficient and controllable sales system.

How you benefit

The aim is to increase the inflow of orders. The sales system focuses the existing competences and capacities upon value-creating activities. Order probabilities are estimated more accurately, resources are used in a more targeted way, the customer recognises more benefit during the offer phase, and the customer relationship and the value of the solution in the context of the customer become the decisive competitive advantage.

In practise, sales teams work on top form; guided well by clear aims, transparency and systematic decisions. The success rate and profit margins increase; the employees find out that it is worth being committed.

Chapter 25: Identifying Non Value Added Tasks Done By Sales Representatives

There are two ways to redesign a process. One option is to start with a "clean piece of paper" and design the process you want. This was popularized in the book "Re-engineering the Corporation" in the early 1990's. It was extremely popular and then fizzled very quickly.

There are many problems with this approach. First, the new process takes too long to design because every step is debated by team members trying to protect their turf. It was not uncommon for re-engineering projects to take 6 months to 2 years to complete. Second, the newly designed process usually did not work because it didn't integrate the company's existing information systems. It is too difficult to start over.

The Lean method is much simpler and faster. We map the current process, then identify and eliminate the non-value-added steps. The new process is simply the old process with the non-value-added steps taken out. Lean projects are completed in 4 weeks and have lasting improvement.

Current State Process Flow Mapping

The sales process of this Distribution Company includes:

131

1. Creating proposals.
2. Configuring orders.
3. Customizing standard product (coming from the manufacturer) to customer specifications.
4. Delivering.
5. Billing.
6. Accounting for payment and paying commission.

We created a process flow map, including all the detailed steps, decisions, paperwork and databases that are part of the Sales Process. The Mapping team included people from each department that touch the process including:
1. Sales Representatives
2. Sales Management
3. Sales Support
4. Parts Department
5. Service Department
6. Accounting

We created a very detailed process flow map to identify all the tasks that are wasting Sales Representatives' time and do not add value to the customer.

Once the Current State Process Flow Map was complete we looked at every step and asked two questions.
1. Does the customer value us doing this step?
2. Is it preventing Sales Representatives from spending more time with customers?

If the task does not add value to the customer, or is preventing Sales Representatives from selling, we considered it a task that should be eliminated or streamlined.

We removed these non-value added tasks from the Process Flow Map and created action items to either eliminate them or reduce the time they require. Then we quantified each step to determine how much time we were saving the Sales Representatives and the Sales Manager. These action items are show below.

Savings for the Sales Manager

1. Sales Manager approves payment to vendors – Should be handled by Accounting (13.8 hours per year saved).
2. Sales Manager Reviews leasing information for Sales Reps – Sales Support can do this (1.7 hours per year).
3. Sales Manager Reviews prep sheet for incomplete information – Should be entered into IT system, not paper, which requires complete information prior to saving (2.5 hours per year).

Savings for the Sales Representatives

1. Sales Reps writing proposals, mailing proposal, filling out vendor-option form, bid info sheet, financing form, mailing contracts, updating used equipment database, completing market share form and proofreading proposals. All of this can be done by Sales Support Admin.

133

2. Sales Reps manually prepare bid based on customer specifications.
3. Use IT System to kick out bid based on Sales Support entering customer specifications.
4. We eliminated 219.8 hours or work per year done by each Sales Representative by eliminating these 10 tasks.

Results

1. Eliminated Sales Representatives doing administrative work by using existing company information systems or moving tasks to Sales Support Admin.
2. Each Sales Representative was given 5.5 weeks of extra selling time per year.
3. Over the following 2 years gross profit margins increased 40%.

This project entailed identifying the non-value-added tasks that Sales Representatives do, and eliminating them or moving them to lower paid sales support personnel. There were 10 tasks a Sales Representative had to do for each customer inquiry that were eliminated from their workload. While this doesn't sound like a significant reduction in steps, we created 5.5 weeks of additional selling time for every Sales Representative.

Sales Representatives should be selling, not doing paperwork. This Lean project freed up time for this company's Sales Representatives to spend more time with customers, understanding their needs, adding more value. The result was that they closed deals at much higher profit margins.

The 40% increase in gross profit margin, happened as sales continued to grow. This equated to a multimillion dollar increase in profit.

Chapter 26: Conclusion

At a recent conference I attended I was reminded of an important point about marketing many of us neglect; namely, that it shouldn't be about selling, or even hyping your company.

Marketing in this era, the speaker explained, should be about taking what others have said about your company and screaming it from the proverbial rooftops, broadcasting that positive buzz to anyone who will listen, typically across direct channels such as social media networks. As he pointed out, it's about finding that one value-driving spark where you are gaining traction and attention in the marketplace and blowing on it until it turns into a roaring fire.

This is critical at a time when the strongest organic sales leads come from prospective clients who hear positive comments about your company from a trusted source, then lean on that endorsement when deciding whether or not to use your service or product. It's about doing less to achieve more, and staying well away from overt sell-marketing tactics that tend to either turn people off or be completely ignored.

Researching how to find those sparks, the consensus answer among entrepreneur friends and colleagues was simple. They told me the best way was to pick up the phone and call every single client I had to get feedback I could use to better define, quantify and eventually promote my company's value propositions and competitive advantage.

Of course, that client feedback research wasn't limited to phone calls or client meetings. It also involved combing social feeds and blogs for positive brand feedback. In the end, the goal is to amplify what is being said about your company to promote your brand in an authentic and effective way.

At AA Global Sourcing, we took this advice and ran with it. We took our entire client list, split it up and began calling each one. We asked each three simple questions: Are you happy with us? Would you recommend us to others? What can we improve upon? The results were game-changing.

Some provided feedback on what we were doing well, while others gave often painful and brutally honest opinions on how they thought we were missing the mark. The latter provided hugely important insight to help improve the way we provide our services. Virtually every instance of negative feedback pointed out the client enjoyed working with AA Global Sourcing, but felt we weren't effectively listening to his or her needs or business objectives. The fact that we took the time to call and understand some of these shortcomings left them feeling relieved we were finally taking steps to become a better service provider.

Once our research was complete, where possible we immediately took action and worked to adjust our service strategy, focusing on everything from frequency of communication to the solutions we offered. That intelligence was funnelled into our marketing materials and initiatives, helping us sell services more effectively by using that positive feedback as a go-to sales tool. This simple process took one week and provided more value than we could have imagined. The best part, it didn't involve implementing an expensive or complex research system. It just took the time to listen.

The experience reminded me that as business owners we are often so blinded by how we think we should be marketing to our clients, that we fail to address their needs, solve a key business problem they might be facing now or in the future, or find innovative new ways to make their work easier and in turn, make their businesses more successful.

Listening is a far more important marketing tool than some loud, irrelevant sales pitch. Like my favourite saying goes: "If you talked to people the way advertisers talked to people, they did punch you in the face."

Good Luck!

Resource and References

Shigeo Shingo, Norman Bodek, Collin McLoughlin: Kaizen and the Art of Creative Thinking - The Scientific Thinking Mechanism

Shigeo Shingo; Fundamental Principles of Lean Manufacturing

Shigeo Shingo, Andrew P. Dillon (Translator); Zero Quality Control: Source Inspection and the Poka-yoke System

Shigeo Shingo; Non-Stock Production: The Shingo System of Continuous Improvement

Shigeo Shingo; A Study of the Toyota Production System from an Industrial Engineering Viewpoint

Shigeo Shingo; A Study of the Toyota Production System from an Industrial Engineering Viewpoint

Drucker, P. (1993) Post-Capitalist Society

Drucker, P., "What Makes an Effective Executive", Harvard Business review, June 2004

Lessons from Toyota's long drive, an interview with Katsuaki Watanabe, HBR, July 2007

Liker, J. & D. Meier, Toyota Talent, McGraw Hill, 2007

Shook, J. , Managing To Learn, Lean Enterprise Institute 2008

Fishman, C., "No Satisfaction", Fast Company, Dec 2006/Jan 2007

Womack, J. & J. Shook, Lean Management and The Role of Lean Leadership, Lean Enterprise Institute presentation, Oct. 2006

www.ingramcontent.com/pod-product-compliance
Lightning Source LLC
Chambersburg PA
CBHW051709170526
45167CB00002B/602